SpringerBriefs in Business

For further volumes:
http://www.springer.com/series/8860

The book is mainly based on the paper: Chiarini, A. (2011). Japanese total quality control, TQM, Deming's system of profound knowledge, BPR, lean and six sigma: Comparison and discussion. *International Journal of Lean Six Sigma*, *2*(4), 332–355

Andrea Chiarini

From Total Quality Control to Lean Six Sigma

Evolution of the Most Important Management Systems for the Excellence

Springer

Andrea Chiarini
Chiarini & Associates
Bologna
Italy

ISSN 2191-5482 ISSN 2191-5490 (electronic)
ISBN 978-88-470-2657-5 ISBN 978-88-470-2658-2 (eBook)
DOI 10.1007/978-88-470-2658-2
Springer Milan Heidelberg New York Dordrecht London

Library of Congress Control Number: 2012935252

Printed on acid-free paper

Springer is part of Springer Science+Business Media (www.springer.com)

Contents

Chapter 1
Introduction

Japanese Total Quality Control (JTQC), Total Quality Management (TQM), Deming's System of Profound Knowledge, Business Process Reengineering (BPR), Lean Thinking and Six Sigma are quality and operations improvement systems all oriented towards process improvement. They have implementation factors and results in common such as: continuous improvement, customer satisfaction, people and management involvement to mention a few. Nonetheless, the systems also present different and important characteristics due to their different origins and the historic path of implementation inside companies.

The literature itself has considered the systems at different times and in different ways. Six Sigma comes from the USA, it is the most recent system, and along with the Japanese Toyota Production System (TPS) revisited by Womack and Jones (1998) with the new name Lean Thinking, it is still extensively researched and discussed by practitioners and academics (Wedgwood 2006). The literature on TQM and JTQC reached a peak in the middle of the 1990s, although less so with TQM but it is still being researched (Osayawe Ehigie and McAndrew 2005). BPR became very popular in the USA in the early 1990s, since then interest in it has decreased and nowadays only the term reengineering has been inherited (Stoica et al. 2004). Deming's system has been analysed and discussed less than the other systems.

In the light of this there is a need to better compare and discuss the evolution of the systems, the ways of implementing them, their distinctions and what they share in common. Indeed the main purpose and contribution of this book lies in the concurrent analysis and classification, by the means of a literature review, of the results and critical implementation factors of the six systems. Deming's Plan-Do-Check-Act (PDCA) model (Deming 1950) has been used to classify the results from the literature review.

The findings will open an interesting debate for future research about the future of the systems and the lessons learnt from their evolutions.

The findings could also be a useful comparison programme for practitioners that want to apply the systems or integrate them.

A. Chiarini, *From Total Quality Control to Lean Six Sigma*, SpringerBriefs in Business,
DOI: 10.1007/978-88-470-2658-2_1, © The Author(s) 2012

References

Deming, W. E. (1950). Elementary principles of the statistical control of quality. Tokyo: JUSE.

Osayawe Ehigie, B., & McAndrew, E. B. (2005). Innovation, diffusion and adoption of total quality management (TQM). *Management Decision, 43*(6), 925–940.

Stoica, M., Chawat, N., & Shin, N. (2004). An investigation of the methodologies of business process reengineering. *International Systems Education Journal, 2*(11), 3–10.

Wedgwood, I. (2006). *Lean sigma, a practitioner's guide*. Upper Saddle River, NJ: Prentice Hall.

Womack, J. P., & Jones, D. T. (1998). *Lean thinking: Banish waste and create wealth in your corporation*. New York: Simon & Schuster.

Chapter 2
A Historical Path of the Systems

In the first years of the 20th century the famous entrepreneur Henry Ford used to say, half serious, half joking, that "Any customer can have a car painted any colour that he wants so long as it is black" and "What doesn't exist cannot break" (referring to a car's optional features). Considering the interruption of the markets development due to the two world wars, in 1960s and 1970s companies all over the world found themselves doing business in a sort of calm sea where the route wasn't difficult to choose. The consumers requested products they did not have which could significantly improve their daily lives and for marketing managers it was relatively simple to satisfy their needs. The post-war generation, for example, used the moped as means of transport, but for obvious reasons desired a car. As soon as they managed to buy one, it became a Sunday morning ritual to tinker away in ones garage, trying to repair and maintain the product, as it was replacing the broken vacuum valve of the black and white television. The washing machine, the television, the fridge, the dishwasher and other objects that we now take for granted, often remained dreams for years for families in the post-war era. As soon as the financial status allowed it the purchase was automatic, without many demands regarding the quality of the product, from those few companies whose main goal was satisfying a rather large local request. In fact, only very few companies tried expanding to foreign markets due to trade protection and communication barriers. Today every company uses the Internet to complete transactions, but to those times even fax did not yet exist. So the consumer bought a product/service that he had never had before, having to choose between a few competing companies; and this product will have definitely changed his lifestyle. In this context it was quite difficult to obtain personalised products, long-term guarantee, immediate delivery and other services that nowadays are ever-present. The production for this market was concentrated on products that scarcely varied,

---

This section is adapted from the first chapter of the book: Chiarini A (2012) Lean Organization, from the Tools of the Toyota Production System to Lean Office. Springer, London.

DOI: 10.1007/978-88-470-2658-2_2, © The Author(s) 2012

produced by few companies that relied on little competition and relatively low-priced raw materials.

So was it really necessary to strive for excellence through quality and by reducing internal waste?

2.1 The Organisational and Productive Model of Mass Production

Between the 19th and the 20th century F.W. Taylor introduced the so-called Scientific Management, reaching the conclusion that the best establishments had to rigidly and scientifically specialize their organizational roles. If the market demanded an increasing quantity of relatively simple products with a constant rhythm, an "organisational clock", which was synchronised with this market, was needed. Rather than having a work forces organized in teams to improve products and processes, it was favoured having work forces concentrating on producing at the right speed and with the correct equipment, leaving the task of finding and removing products not up to standard at the end of the chain to quality inspectors. Scientific Management is the organizational model used by Ford to produce the famous model "T", introducing the assembly line. Compared to taylorism, Ford even believed that the worker had to be completely subdued by the mechanism of the chain: the assembly line set the rhythm of production, or, as we nowadays call it, takt time (cycle time) and the worker had to comply without questioning. A perfect model, with an uninterrupted lead-time would certainly not lead to warehouses with a low inventory turnover. And what about employee management? Concepts like Team Building, Job Enrichment & Rotation and self-accountability were not applied; in fact, workers often felt alienated in this system, an aspect discussed in Charlie Chaplin's famous film "Modern Times"; even the quality of products was not exactly up to Six Sigma standards, since these were checked by production line inspectors.

To be fair, this organisation allowed a considerable reduction of the car's unit price, and Ford started selling the cars to the workers, who in the meantime saw their purchasing power rise thanks to the parallel increase of the gross domestic product.

2.2 The Birth of the Japanese Management Systems

Some authors describe the dawn of the Japanese industrial system almost like a philosophical myth; a concoction of elements connected to the rigid social system, the comparison between Shinto and the western philosophy of Cartesian origin, lead to the success we now know. Historical anecdotes aside, analysing the situation with the eye of a macro-economist, it's certain that Japan, in the mass production glory years, emerged defeated from the second-world war and had to fight obstacles that western, especially American, industries did not have. It's common knowledge that post world war Japan had:

- higher raw material costs: since Japan has few natural resources, these have to be imported;
- rigid salary ranges due to a stifling union system imposed by the victorious Americans;
- a smaller internal demand compared to western countries, considering the difficulties induced by economic crisis after the defeat in the Second World War.

Attracted by mass production, which kept the western industries at high speed, the inventors of TQC and Lean Manufacturing attempted to compete with similar products obtaining poor results. Mass production followed the very simple equation of "quality equal to costs", and since the Japanese had the initial disadvantage of elevated costs, there was high risk of producing products of poorer quality than the western competitors. Someone may still remembers the Japanese products of the 1960s, like cameras of very poor quality quite similar to the Chinese products of the late 80s. There are many myths regarding the famous journey in 1950 of the Toyota heir, Eiji Toyoda, and his production manager, Taiichi Ohno, to Ford to understand how they could apply mass production methods to Toyota. Ohno understood immediately that it would not have been a success due to the aforementioned problems; instead, they would have to thoroughly modify the cost structure to obtain a necessary cost reduction. Meanwhile, the situation on the international markets was rapidly changing, moving away from the organisational structures of mass production.

2.3 The Relentless Decline of Mass Production in the Western Nations

In the first years of the 1970s, the GDP of the industrialised western nations was still increasing steadily, and with them, the purchasing power of the consumers.

It has been sociologically proven that an increase of purchasing power is accompanied by an inevitable tendency of the consumer to demand higher quality, seen as reliability, personalized products and other bonuses. Thus, the consumer starts to complicate the lives of marketing managers and their companies by demanding diverse products and thus causing an explosion of production codes.

American and European reached mass product saturation at the end of the 1960s, which reached its peak in 1971 with the American economic crisis and Nixon stepping back on the 1944 Bretton Woods system that determined the convertibility of dollars to gold.

Parallel to this important historical event, the Arab–Israeli Yom Kippur war in 1973 caused increase of petroleum and natural gas prices of 70%. These political and economical events clawed at the heart of Ford concept: the concept of unlimited development based on the limited and unstable resource that is petroleum.

Thus the Japanese industry and especially Toyota in the 70s and 80s had a head start in competing in this new big economic scene, since they had already developed strategies and methods of eliminating internal waste (the famous Muda), improving the quality of products and, especially, reacting to new clients that demanded personalised products at competitive prices. By the end of the 1970s Japan was the nation to follow for its industrial and economic structure, and many economists were certain that the American decline was inevitable in the next decades.

The western answer to this new situation, it must be said, was not particularly speedy. European countries, for example, tended towards protectionism, leading to a general delay in development, and some organisations were still trailing behind in the new millennium. Differently, the USA initially responded with a reorganisation policy based on cutting back directly on production costs, especially labour and, at the same time, increasing automation.

In the 80s, aided by the explosion of computer science in companies, the concept of Computer Integrated Manufacturing (CIM) is introduced in the USA, making it clear that mainframe, server, robotised cells and AGV would have replaced workmen bit by bit and led to a workman-free factory controlled by few, specialised technicians. Thanks the best universities in the world such as MIT, Harvard, Stanford and others, the USA tried to respond to this new situations with the most advanced systems of planning and control. Software such as MRP I (Material Requirements Planning) and MRP II (Manufacturing Resources Planning), still much used today, are developed together with the first mainframes and servers for companies, making it possible, by using predictive models, to partially keep up with the increase of codes and the reduction of lots the market clamoured for.

2.4 The Recovery of the USA in the 1980s–1990s and the Proclamation of the Japanese Production Systems

It is important to realise that the USA responded to the crisis with a revolution of their economical and industrial philosophy. Obviously a system that leads to excellence like Lean Manufacturing, Six Sigma or for instance TQM (Total Quality Management) has to start with significant commitment by the leadership. The USA started off with a liberal breeze brought by president Ronald Reagan from 1981 to 1989, who personally handed over the Malcom Baldridge prize to companies of excellence; this was the sign of a new era. Even Hollywood declared that the era of finance and of those that considered companies mere short-term profit centres had come to an end, and that now it was time for engineers concentrated on processes; Oliver Stone, the American film director, in the film Wall Street denounced greed (greed is good) and the absence of rules in a world of bankers that would have soon been surpassed by technicians and managers that believed in production. In many ways a similar scenario to the last economic crisis that was set off by large banks going bankrupt as well as the US and European public debts is underpinned on the not long-view of short term profits.

Still in the 1980s, Deming wrote one of the best books on management of the last two decades, “Out of the Crisis”: a symbolic title that warned and advised the whole industrial world what really needed to be done to survive in the competitive struggle. A shame, really, that the last crisis didn’t produce similar masterpieces.

The American economy took off and the global competition became more intense. In the 1980s the strategies necessary to compete increased in number:

- understanding the customers demand (Voice of the customer);
- understanding when to introduce new products/services (Time to market);
- the safety and reliability of a product;
- the mix of codes and subsequent reduction of lots in sale and supply;
- on-time delivery;
- reduction of production costs;
- the total cost of a product or service.

As well as the stress on automation and on computerised systems, the USA also started importing TQC-TQM and Lean Manufacturing principles. Womack and Jones of MIT published a book in 1989 called The Machine That Changed the World, introducing the concept of Lean Thinking in contrast with Mass production. This book, together with the sequel Lean Thinking, finally proclaimed the success of Lean in the whole world. Lean Manufacturing or Toyota Production System, of pure Japanese origin, became a necessity to compete with another important system that was developed in the early 1990s branching from TQM as many authors suggested: Six Sigma.

2.5 The American Model of Six Sigma

From 1985 to the early 1990s Motorola experimented with the famous Six Sigma pattern first on productive processes, subsequently on all company processes, saving 1.5 billion dollars in 5 years and winning the Malcom Balbridge award. Six Sigma spread to most of the western world in the early years of the new millennium, thanks to Motorola and especially General Electrics (GE) and its famous CEO Jack Welch. GE gave Six Sigma that strategic dimension that made it to system of excellence; removing the image it had of being a set of tools to improve quality.

In the year 2000 Harry and Schroeder published a famous book on Six Sigma, giving to this management system a precise route that starts with strategies, uses teams with certified specialization and improvement programs organized in 5 steps (Define-Measure-Analyse-Improve-Control or DMAIC) and, especially, delivers results in the form of saving.

The main principle of Six Sigma is reducing the variability of processes. Every process, be it productive or of service, ideally has a target. A polished steel pole must have a certain diameter, like taking care of a financial case must not take more than a certain amount of days. Unfortunately, processes are by nature subject to variability and so results drift away from target. Within the process there are certain traits critical to reaching the target that need to remain within a certain programmed toleration zone. For example, to avoid hospital-induced infections a certain bacterial load has to be present. These critical characteristics to the quality of the product/service in Six Sigma are called Critical To Quality, or CTQ. The deviation from the CTQs is statistically measured through the "sigma", better known as standard deviation. In general the bigger the number of sigma inside the range around the target, the smaller the possibility of producing non-conformities. Which easily translates into satisfied customers and saving in terms of Cost Of Poor Quality (COPQ). If a process reaches a six sigma quality, this means that this process will produce 3.4 defect products or service per million; an unexceptional quality when talking about clothes, but an unacceptable one when discussing airplane landings or surgery success.

Chapter 3
Literature Review Concerning the Comparison of the Systems

A few authors have investigated two, three or four of the mentioned systems but no authors have compared JTQC, TQM, Deming's system, Lean, BPR and Six Sigma at the same time.

Very few articles analysed Deming's system trying to compare it with other systems; the only interesting articles have been written by Gitlow (1994, 1995). Gitlow compared JTQC and Deming's system in detail, finding several points of agreement and disagreement between the two systems. Unfortunately the author limited his research to the two systems.

Martinez-Lorente et al. (1998) compared American and Japanese TQC with TQM. The paper is an interesting analysis of differences between American and Japanese ways of implementing the systems. For the authors the differences are linked to culture, politics and company philosophy. The professionalism and specialisation, high turnover rates, easy layoffs and short-term profits of the Taylor's system are the external factors that have created a different approach in the USA.

Ricondo and Viles (2005) wrote the most extensive paper in terms of comparisons. Lean, Six Sigma, TQM, reengineering (BPR) and learning organisation are compared at the same time. In an interesting way they found that many quality tools and techniques are shared by all the approaches, such as the seven basic tools, the seven management tools, Statistical Process Control (SPC), benchmarking, teamwork and brainstorming, to mention the most important. The authors also found that each system has its own specific tools and techniques such as kanban for Lean Organisation, Information Technology (IT) tools for BPR and statistical tools for TQM and Six Sigma.

Dahlgaard and Dahlgaard-Park (2006) tried to compare the principles and results of Lean Production, Six Sigma quality and TQM. Some foregone conclusions emerged such as Lean and TQM had developed from Japanese practices. In a more original way the authors claim that Lean Production and Six Sigma are new alternative TQM roadmaps, even if there is not any specific validation of this issue in the paper.

More recently Johannsen (2011) wrote a paper dedicated to state-of-the-art integration in quality management and pointed out that there is a lack of guidelines

A. Chiarini, *From Total Quality Control to Lean Six Sigma*, SpringerBriefs in Business,
DOI: 10.1007/978-88-470-2658-2_3, © The Author(s) 2012

for integrating Lean Management, Six Sigma and TQM. The results are more a research agenda for the future than a point of view concerning what are the common characteristics and the differences.

To sum up, the authors have analysed some, but not all, of the systems, identifying differences in terms of origin, culture, tools and techniques and other factors. However, there is a lack of an accurate comparison among all the six systems in order to understand the common results and critical implementation factors, their differences and whether some of them can be an alternative to the others.

References

Dahlgaard, J. J., & Dahlgaard-Park, S. M. (2006). Lean production, six sigma quality, TQM and company culture. *The TQM Magazine, 18*(3), 263–281.

Gitlow, H. (1994). A comparison of Japanese total quality control and Deming's theory of management. *The American Statistician, 48*(3), 197–203.

Gitlow, H. (1995). Understanding total quality creation (TQC): The Japanese school of thought. *Quality Engineering, 7*(3), 523–542.

Johannsen, F. (2011). *State of the art concerning the integration of methods and techniques in quality management—literature review and an agenda for research.* European Conference on Information Systems (ECIS) 2011 Proceedings. Paper 41.

Martinez-Lorente, A. R., Dewhurst, F., & Dale, B. G. (1998). Total quality management: Origins and evolution of the term. *The TQM Magazine, 10*(5), 378–386.

Ricondo, I., & Viles, E. (2005). Six sigma and its link to TQM, BPR, lean and the learning organisation. *International Journal of Six Sigma and Competitive Advantage, 1*(3), 323–354.

Chapter 4
Research Methodology

The research methodology is based on a literature review. In the literature there is neither an academic discussion nor case studies carried out by practitioners concerning the six systems at the same time. Therefore the research is firstly based on a literature review of each single system trying subsequently to compare the findings. This specific comparison is structured following the PDCA cycle as a way of implementing the systems top-down and bottom-up. As several papers suggested, PDCA can be successfully used as a framework for implementing different management systems.

Deming's system naturally has the PDCA cycle in its DNA. Ishikawa (1985) slightly redefined the PDCA cycle in order to include goals, targets, methods for reaching them as well as training and education (Moen and Norman 2006). Deming's PDCA can surely be considered the most common pattern inside TQM (Cheng 2008). Linderman et al. (2003) for instance suggested that in case of process improvement Six Sigma is patterned after the PDCA cycle. Lucas (2002) found that Six Sigma uses a modified PDCA management cycle. Cheng (2008) and Graves et al. (2000) discussed that Six Sigma and TQM are based on a PDCA management cycle. Dennis and Shoot (2007) analysed PDCA as a methodology and cornerstone for Lean. BPR is not directly linked to PDCA, however, its way of implementing can be associated with it. For instance, Muthu et al. (1999) introduced five steps to implement BPR, similar to PDCA, as discussed in the BPR section.

The Plan stage is usually dedicated to the strategies, the definition of the objectives (Kondo 1998; Tani 1995; Ramsey et al. 2001) and the design of the organisation, including in part human resources management (Conti 1997).

The Do stage is considered the implementation phase from the voice of the customer capture until the delivery of the product/service (Conti 1997). Ishikawa (1985) used to include training and education in the Do stage. In the Check and

---

This section and the followings are adapted from the paper: Chiarini (2011).

A. Chiarini, *From Total Quality Control to Lean Six Sigma*, SpringerBriefs in Business,
DOI: 10.1007/978-88-470-2658-2_4,

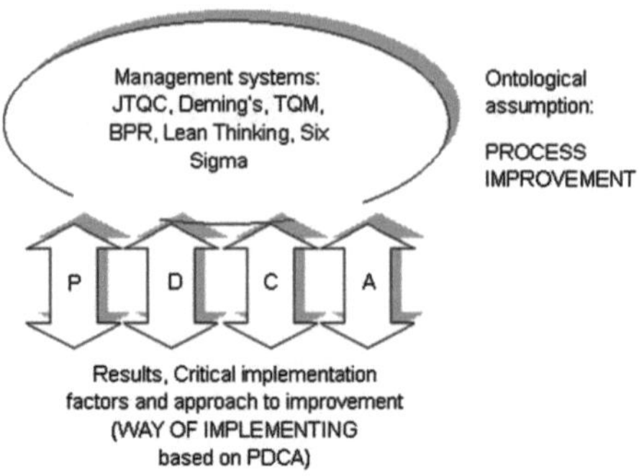

Fig. 4.1 Ontological assumption and way of implementing for the systems

Act stages the organisation checks to evaluate how it conforms to the Plan stage and Acts on what has been learned (Johnson 2002).

In the discussion section, the findings of the literature review will be summarised and compared with each other within the PDCA cycle in order to obtain for the six systems the results and their critical implementation factors.

These latter, as shown in Fig. 4.1, are considered to be the way of implementing the systems to achieve the same fundamental target: process improvement. Although the objective of this paper is not to go into philosophical discussions, process improvement can be ontologically considered the nature of being (Hirschheim et al. 1995) of the six systems.

References

Cheng, J. L. (2008). Implementing six sigma via TQM improvement: An empirical study in Taiwan. *The TQM Journal, 20*(3), 182–195.

Chiarini, A. (2011). Japanese total quality control, TQM, Deming's system of profound knowledge, BPR, lean and six sigma: Comparison and discussion. *International Journal of Lean Six Sigma, 2*(4), 332–355.

Conti, T. (1997). Total quality management. *Total Quality Management and Business Excellence, 8*(2–3), 5–15.

Dennis, P., & Shook, J. (2007). *Lean production simplified: A plain language guide to the world's most powerful production systems*. New York: Productivity Press.

Graves, S. C., Gershwin, S., & Popoola, O. A. (2000). Development of a methodology for the rapid implementation of a sustainable lean manufacturing system. Available at: http://dspace.mit.edu/handle/1721.1/9000. Accessed 3 Aug 2011.

Hirschheim, R., Klein, H., & Lyytinen, K. (1995). *International systems development and data modeling. Conceptual foundations and philosophical foundations*. Cambridge, UK: Cambridge University Press.

Ishikawa, K. (1985). *What is total quality control? The Japanese way*. Englewood Cliffs, NJ: Prentice-Hall.

Johnson, C. N. (2002). The benefits of PDCA. *Quality Progress, 35*, 120–121.

Kondo, Y. (1998). Hoshin kanri-a participative way of quality management in Japan. *The TQM Magazine, 10*(6), 425–431.

Linderman, K., Schroeder, R. G., Zaheer, S., & Choo, A. S. (2003). Six sigma: A goaltheoretic perspective. *Journal of Operations Management, 3*(21), 193–203.
Lucas, M. L. (2002). The essential of six sigma: How successful six sigma implementation can improve the bottom line. *Quality Progress, 35*(1), 27–31.
Moen, R., & Norman, C. (2006). Evolution of the PDCA cycle. Available at: http://pkpinc.com/files/NA01MoenNormanFullpaper.pdf. Accessed 3 Aug 2011.
Muthu, S., Whitman, L., & Hossein, S. C. (1999). *Business process reengineering: A consolidated methodology*. Proceedings of the 4th Annual International Conference on Industrial Engineering Theory, Applications, and Practice, Department of the Interior Enterprise Architecture, U.S.
Ramsey, C., Ormsby, S., & Marsch, T. (2001). Performance-improvement strategies can reduce costs. *Healthcare Financial Management*, (*Supplement*), pp. 2–6.
Tani, T. (1995). Interactive control in target cost management. *Management Accounting Research, 6*(4), 399–414.

Chapter 5
Japanese Total Quality Control

TQC is surely the oldest system and its roots sink into the earliest statistical research carried out by Shewart (1939). These principles were further developed in Japan after the end of the Second World War. Feigenbaum developed TQC, defining it as (1961, p. 6): "A network of the management/control and procedure that is required to produce and deliver a product with a specific quality standard".

It can be noted that Feigenbaum's definition of TQC was focused on the so-called quality assurance that implies respect of standards, procedures, work instructions to reach above all effectiveness for the customer (Ishikawa 1985).

TQC in Japan evolved into Company Wide Quality Control mainly due to Ishikawa (1985), leading TQC towards the so-called Japanese TQC (JTQC).

According to Ishikawa (1985), TQC tries to optimise cost-effectiveness and usefulness, while satisfying customers at the same time. The same results can be found in Kano (1993): he clearly stated (p. 13) that the purpose is to increase 'customer satisfaction and quality assurance'.

Ishikawa (1985), King (1989) and Mizuno (1988) analysed the Plan stage which in its strategic dimension is based on policy management and is known as hoshin kanri. Kano (1993) strongly believed that top management should create the right energy and motivation to promote and sustain quality.

Iizuka and Osada (1988) and Ishikawa (1985) discussed participatory management and the humanistic view of the worker in JTQC. Promotional activities or administrative systems (Gitlow 1995) are the 'vehicles' of JTQC for managing the organisation and all the employees. JTQC has principles such as daily management, cross-functional management, voluntary quality control circle and training. Daily management is based on the improvement of best-practice methods and the quality control circle operates day by day involving all the levels and employees. Kano et al. (1984) pointed out how a quality circle should be underpinned by respect of humanity, building a bright and enjoyable workshop environment that improves without limits human potential. Furthermore, Ishikawa (1985) considered that TQC was not exclusively a task for quality specialists, even though people have to receive training and education for the best practices. By contrast, Feigenbaum (1961), more representative of the

A. Chiarini, *From Total Quality Control to Lean Six Sigma*, SpringerBriefs in Business,
DOI: 10.1007/978-88-470-2658-2_5, © The Author(s) 2012

American approach, discussed how quality control needed a particular specialisation of some figures and departments.

In the Do stage, Ishikawa (1985), Iizuka and Osada (1988), Kano et al. (1984) agreed that having a customer orientation, where the customer can also be considered the next process, is a fundamental pillar of JTQC. The quality circles, along with the management, are supposed to manage processes by fact, achieving targets that can include quality, cost, scheduling, quantity, sales and profit and safety. Ishikawa (1985), in particular, stressed the use of the seven basic tools such as check sheets, Pareto, histograms, stratification, control charts, cause-and-effect diagrams and interrelationship diagraphs. However, depending on the problem, management tools and advanced ones such as design of experiments, quality function deployment, Taguchi and many others can be applied. Some tools that typically are classified within Lean Thinking are also used inside quality circles. For instance mistake proofing or poka-yoke systems along with 5S and Cleanliness, Arrangement, Neatness, Discipline and Orderliness (CANDO) can be traced to JTQC (Shingo 1986, 1989).

In the literature concerning JTQC there is no evidence of any particular way of reporting and controlling the results achieved by quality circles. Ishikawa (1985) pointed out how the results in general are measured by indicators, linked in particular to product conformity. Reactions to nonconformities are managed by corrective actions and problem solving. Audits can be led to control and check the quality assurance system (Gitlow 1995). Lessons acquired from corrective actions can be carried out in other similar processes by the means of preventive actions. Mizuno (1988) explained how the results from the corrective and preventive actions can become inputs in the hoshin kanri system for the Act stage.

References

Feigenbaum, A. V. (1961). *Total quality control*. New York: McGraw-Hill.

Gitlow, H. (1995). Understanding total quality creation (TQC): The Japanese school of thought. *Quality Engineering, 7*(3), 523–542.

Iizuka, Y., & Osada, H. (1988). *JTQC in Japan today*. MN: Process Management Institute St. Paul.

Ishikawa, K. (1985). *What is total quality control? The Japanese way*. Englewood Cliffs, NJ: Prentice-Hall.

Kano, N. (1993). A perspective on quality activities in American firms. *California Management Review, 35*(3), 12–31.

Kano, N., Seraku, N., Takahashi, F., & Tsuji, S. (1984). Attractive quality and must-be quality, *Hinshitsu. The Journal of the Japanese Society for Quality Control*, pp. 39–48 (April).

King, R. (1989). *Hoshin planning: The development approach*. MA: GOAL/QPC, Methuen.

Mizuno, S. (1988). *Management for quality improvement: The 7 new QC tools*. Cambridge, MA: Productivity Press.

Shewart, W. A. (1939). *Statistical method from the viewpoint of quality control*. Washington, DC: The Graduate School the Department of Agriculture.

Shingo, S. (1986). *Zero quality control: Source inspection and the poka-yoke system study*. Cambridge, MA: Productivity Press.

Shingo, S. (1989). *A study of the Toyota production system from an industrial engineering viewpoint*. Cambridge, MA: Productivity Press.

Chapter 6
Total Quality Management

As previously discussed, Japanese companies have developed TQC mainly using the teachings of Ishikawa, Deming and Juran. Feigenbuam was the first to use the term TQC but he started introducing differences between American and Japanese TQC these differences have been extended by TQM.

Ishikawa shifted the attention from the term 'control' to 'management'. According to Martinez-Lorente et al. (1998), in the literature the idea began that quality does not just have to be controlled but managed. Probably this was the actual beginning of the TQM movement and principles. According to several authors (Grant et al. 1994; Milakovich 1991; Ehigie and Akpan 2004), Deming was one of the founders of TQM, launching it in the world through the book Out of the Crisis (1986).

One of the most interesting aspect of TQM surely was the definition and classification of the 'poor-quality cost', mainly due to Harrington (1986). The Six Sigma COPQ (Cost of Poor Quality) classification is quite similar to Harrington's original classification. The 'hidden factory' is a well-known subject of discussion for everyone who deals with Six Sigma, TQM, or even with the ISO 9001 certification.

Whenever products or services do not satisfy requirements set by customers or by the organization itself, a non-conformity is generated, with its related Costs Of Poor Quality, classified as following:

- prevention and appraisal costs;
- internal and external defectiveness.

Therefore the hidden factory is the factory where people rework product/services and redo activities. To reduce the aforementioned costs, extra focus must be concentrated on prevention investments, to which the investment costs of managing Kaizen team must be added. Table 6.1 lists most of the items connected to the aforementioned categories.

The COPQ are divided in internal and external costs, depending on when they are identified (internally or by a customer), but the company also has appraisal costs, which, against common belief, are not really useful and usually hide other problems and decrease value added. The cost of the incoming inspection of materials from suppliers, for example, often compensates for the poor quality of

A. Chiarini, *From Total Quality Control to Lean Six Sigma*, SpringerBriefs in Business,
DOI: 10.1007/978-88-470-2658-2_6,

the supplier's work. Basically, the seven types of waste described by Lean can be found within the categories of internal defectiveness.

Nowadays there is a huge quantity of literature about TQM but, according to Knights and Willmott (2000), sometimes authors contradict each other and it is not clear what TQM contains. The literature shows confusion beginning from the management styles and their strategies. An interesting paper by Chatterjee and Yilmaz (1993 p. 16) points out how TQM gurus such as Deming, Juran and Crosby did not agree on quality strategies.

> … Deming is strongly opposed to management by objectives… Crosby recommended zero defects as a quality objective… Juran and Deming are against this because the inherent variability in all processes…

However, senior managers should be very involved and the most important critical characteristic for TQM implementation in the West seems to be management behaviour and participation, management by fact and long-term vision Porter and Parker (1993). A steering committee of senior managers normally leads the implementation programme. TQM focuses on quality performances, such as Costs of Poor Quality (COPQ), although in the literature cases of integration between TQM and Corporate Social Responsibility (CSR) (McAdam and Leonard 2003; Zink 2007; Meehan et al. 2006) and TQM and environmental aspects (Kitazawa and Sarkis 2000; Daily and Huang 2001; Miles and Russel 1997) are frequent. Hoshin kanri in TQM is still one of the most used strategic systems (Akao 2004) in Japan, even though TQM is also associated with the American Balanced Scorecard and other deployment systems (Hoque 2003).

In terms of human resources, TQM stresses the use of team building and team efforts (Ross 1993; Spector and Beer 1994; Bubshait and Farooq 1999) and employee involvement is mandatory. During the 1980s, in TQM and JTQC, implementation at the bottom level was carried out through quality circles. Unfortunately, quality circles failed in many Western companies as described by Hayward et al. (1985) and Drago (1988) and companies had to think about different improvement teams. The reasons lie, first, in weak senior managers' leadership, and second in nonparticipation and once more in an unclear connection with company strategies

In the Do stage, voice of the customer capture as well as basic and advanced statistical tools are fundamental to improvement projects and no author criticised them. Sila and Ebrahimpur (2002) investigated critical factors of TQM concluding that, in the literature written in English until 2000, TQM had been studied in dozen of ways grouped into 25 categories. The authors outlined how TQM has also been influenced by national awards such as the Malcolm Baldridge and the European Foundation for Quality Management award. For instance benchmarking and self-assessment are largely used and derived from this field.

Finally it seems that Western TQM in the course of time is losing its identity. In reviewing papers (Saylor 1992; Pike and Barns 1993; Ross 1993; Zairi et al. 1994; Omachonu and Ross 1994 ; George and Weimerskirch 1998) it can be found that many improvement projects have been carried out under the TQM 'umbrella' but

Table 6.1 Prevention, appraisal and defectiveness costs

Prevention costs (Investments)
Improvement programs (Kaizen Workshops for Lean, Six Sigma teams, TQM teams for improvement, etc.)
Quality management staff (not including quality inspection)
Quality management software, ERP costs
Quality management and laboratory instrumentation amortization (Research and Development, prototypes, preventive tests, etc.)
External laboratories for preventive checks
Penalties for damage responsibility for defect products
Process identification, process management documentation
Training and creating awareness
External consultancies for Lean Six Sigma
Defining targets and goals for improvement
Quality planning
Data analysis and system reviewing
Measuring customer satisfaction
Measuring processes and self-assessment
QFD, FMEA and FTA processes, defining reliability goals, reviewing and checking design and development, DFM, DFA etc.
Product risk management
New product approval process
SPC management
Design of experiments
Preventive and predictive maintenance
Preventive supplier assessment
Identification and traceability of products
Studying reproducibility and repeatability of measures
Problem solving and managing preventive actions
Appraisal costs
Testing and inspection staff
Measuring equipment and device calibration staff
Measuring equipment and device amortization
Inspection software
External laboratories
Third party certifications
Incoming test and inspection
Inspections during production
Final inspection
Conducting internal inspection visits
Conducting inspection visits of suppliers to maintain qualification
Calibration and management of measuring equipment

Internal defectiveness (including Lean wastes)
Staff who manage defects
Amortization of equipment and machines dedicated to rework
Product rework
Scraps

(continued)

Table 6.1 (continued)

Internal defectiveness (including Lean wastes)
Depreciation of products or services
Selecting and rechecking products
Management of corrective actions
Breakdowns, small stops, reduced speed
Setup and adjustments
Increase in stock and handling costs
Excess of motions
Surpluses or shortages of staff, excessive turnover, absenteeism
Conducting inspections/audit after the production of non-conformities
Conducting inspections/audit after supplier non-conformities
Accidents at work
Environmental accidents
External defectiveness costs
Loss of customer revenue
Management of complaints and returned products
Reworking, reassembling, selecting and rechecking products from customers
Penalties for non-conformities
Legal actions
Management of products in warranty
Product recall

without a similar pattern. Paton (1994) even defined TQM as a philosophy not a science and as such it cannot be developed through a precise roadmap or pattern. Hellsten and Klefsjö (2000) found that the 'fathers' of TQM sometimes do not like the concept. Furthermore, the same authors found that the same TQM concept could have different names and that there are vague descriptions and few definitions of TQM. However it seems that in Japan TQM still has its own identity, strictly linked to JTQC (Yamaji and Amasaka 2008); other Eastern countries also recognise that there is a successful Japanese TQM style that can be followed (Nassir Shaari 2010).

References

Akao, Y. (2004). *Hoshin Kanri: Policy deployment for successful TQM*. New York: Productivity Press.

Bubshait, A., & Farooq, G. (1999). Team building and project success. *Cost engineering, 41*(7), 34–38.

Chatterjee, S., & Yilmaz, M. (1993). Quality confusion: too many gurus, not enough disciples. *Business Horizons, 36*(3), 15–18.

Daily, B. F., & Huang, S. (2001). Achieving sustainability through attention to human resource factors in environmental management. *International Journal of Operations and Productions Management, 21*(12), 1539–1552.

Deming, W. E. (1986). *Out of the crisis*. Boston, MA: MIT Press.

Drago, R. (1988). Quality circle survival: An exploratory analysis. *Industrial Relations: A Journal of Economy and Society, 27*(3), 336–351.

Ehigie, B. O., & Akpan, R. C. (2004). Roles of perceived leadership styles and rewards in the practice of total quality management. *Leadership & Organization Development Journal, 25*(1), 24–40.

George, S., & Weimerskirch, A. (1998). *Total quality management: Strategies and techniques proven at today's most successful companies*. New York: Wiley and Son.

Grant, R., Shani, R., & Krishnan, R. (1994). TQM's challenge to management theory and practice. *Sloan Management Review, 35*(2), 25–36.

Harrington, H. J. (1986). *Poor-quality cost*. Milwaukee: ASQ Quality Press.

Hayward, S. G., Dale, B. G., & Fraser, V. C. M. (1985). Quality circle failure and how to avoid it. *European Management Journal, 3*(2), 103–111.

Hellsten, U., & Klefsjö, B. (2000). TQM as a management system consisting of values, techniques and tools. *The TQM Magazine, 12*(4), 238–244.

Hoque, Z. (2003). Total quality management and the balanced scorecard approach: A critical analysis of their potential relationships and directions for research. *Critical Perspectives on Accounting, 14*(5), 553–566.

Kitazawa, S., & Sarkis, J. (2000). The relationship between ISO 14001 and continuous source reduction programs. *International Journal of Operations and Production Management, 20*(2), 225–248.

Knights, D., & Wilmott, H. (2000). *The reengineering revolution?: Critical studies of corporate change*. London: Sage.

Martinez-Lorente, A. R., Dewhurst, F., & Dale, B. G. (1998). Total quality management: Origins and evolution of the term. *The TQM Magazine, 10*(5), 378–386.

McAdam, R., & Leonard, D. (2003). Corporate social responsibility in a total quality management context: opportunities for sustainable growth. *Corporate Governance, 3*(4), 36–45.

Meehan, J., Meehan, K., & Richards, A. (2006). Corporate social responsibility: The 3C-SR model. *International Journal of Social Economics, 33*(5/6), 386–398.

Milakovich, M. E. (1991). Total quality management in the public sector. *National Productivity Review, 10*(2), 195–213.

Miles, M. P., & Russell, G. R. (1997). ISO 14000 total environmental management: the integration of environmental marketing, total quality management, and corporate environmental policy. *Journal Of Quality Management, 2*(1), 151–168.

Nassir Shaari, J. A. (2010). Barriers to implement TQM in Japanese way: A study on companies in Malasya. *International Review of Business Research Papers, 6*(5), 400–410.

Omachonu, V. K., & Ross, J. E. (1994). *Principles of total quality*. Delray Beach: St. Lucie Press.

Paton, S.M. (1994). Is TQM dead?, Quality Digest Magazine, April 1994, pp. 1–5.

Pike, J., & Barns, R. (1993). *TQM in action*. London: Chapman and Hall.

Porter, M., & Parker, (1993). Total quality management, the critical success factors. *Total Quality Management & Business Excellence, 4*(1), 13–22.

Ross, J. E. (1993). *Total quality management: Text, cases, and readings*. Delray Beach: St. Lucie Press.

Saylor, J. H. (1992). *TQM field manual*. New York: McGraw-Hill.

Sila, I. and Ebrahimpor, M. (2002). An investigation of the total quality management survey based research between 1989 and 2000: A literature review, *The International Journal of Quality and Reliability Management*, Vol. 19, Iss. 6/7, pp. 902–971.

Spector, B., & Beer, M. (1994). Beyond TQM programmes. *Journal of Organizational Change Management, 7*(2), 63–70.

Yamaji, M., & Amasaka, K. (2008). New Japan quality management model: implementation of new jit for strategic management technology. *International Business & Economics Research Journal, 7*(3), 107–114.

Zairi, M., Letza, S. R., & Oakland, J. S. (1994). Does TQM impact on bottom-line results? *The TQM Magazine, 6*(1), 38–43.

Zink, K. J. (2007). From total quality management to corporate sustainability based on a stakeholder management. *Journal of Management History, 13*(4), 394–401.

Chapter 7
Deming's System of Profound Knowledge

Deming's system is based on the Deming's last book The New Economics: For Industry, Government, Education edited in 1993 and following the masterpiece Out of the Crisis published in 1986. As previously stated, Deming is unanimously considered one of the fathers of TQM and his works are widely known and quoted. However, there are few articles and case studies about Deming's System of Profound Knowledge and its implementation.

The system is divided in four interdependent parts: appreciation of a system, theory of variation, theory of knowledge and psychology. A system is broken down into several components and the management has the responsibility of heading the components in the same way. Within the system there are two causes of variation, special and system causes. Employees and technicians have to find and resolve the causes. Knowledge should be based on a theory and managers, by the means of theory, have to predict the future events starting from the past. There is no truth, theory can be reviewed and changed. Psychology helps to understand employees, their interactions and the interactions with the system. Management must understand intrinsic and extrinsic motivation as well as over justification (Gitlow 1994).

Deming (1993), in the Plan stage, criticised the practice of management by objectives: it does not lead towards results for the entire system and all the stakeholders. Management should not privilege one or few stakeholders. Employees, customers, suppliers, stockholders, the community and even the competitors should receive welfare from the company in the long term. Deming stated (1993, p. 2): "A product or service possesses quality if it helps somebody and enjoys a good and sustainable market".

In Deming's system there is no trace of particular processes in order to deploy objectives and goals. In any case, Deming claimed that methods are more important than goals and targets. Many negative cases of defined targets that are reached but reached in wrong ways are analysed in the second chapter 'The heavy losses' of his book. The long-term process is named by Deming 'analytic management' and it is in contrast to the short-term results-only orientation, named 'enumerative management'.

A. Chiarini, *From Total Quality Control to Lean Six Sigma*, SpringerBriefs in Business, DOI: 10.1007/978-88-470-2658-2_7, © The Author(s) 2012

Management must promote and create a balance of intrinsic and extrinsic motivation (Gitlow 1994). This can be considered one of the most interesting and characteristic elements of the system. The energy released by intrinsic motivations is, by far, more positive for improving processes and employees, and in this way their potential and joy of working shines. A win–win environment is fundamental to stakeholders, including employees. A cooperative environment has to be preferred by management instead of a competitive environment. Competition can lead people and departments to reach their own goals and not the goals of the entire system. According to Gitlow (1994), the pursuit of customer satisfaction is internally motivated as well and in any case cannot be achieved without regard to the stakeholders' needs.

In the Do stage Deming's system does not emphasise any particular tool or group such as advanced statistical tools. Each organisation can choose its tools for reducing variation. Anyway, Deming believes in the tools and techniques of quality management and Shewart (1939) and his tools are often quoted.

Managers must not introduce a fear climate inside the organisation, and performance check processes that introduce ranking of employees or departments are not the best for Deming (Gitlow 1994). Instead, it is vital for a manager to learn the psychology of individuals, to spend time listening to them and understand why they failed. Variation has to be measured and continually reduced, and the theory which underpins the system periodically revised on the basis of its capacity to predict the future.

As Deming himself said (1993, p. 66): "the book is for people who are living under the tyranny of the prevailing style of management" and in this way it can be considered a behavioural guideline for managers, especially in the USA.

References

Deming, W. E. (1993). *The new economics: For industry, Government, Education.* Cambridge, MA: MIT, Center for Advanced Engineering Study.

Gitlow, H. (1994). A comparison of Japanese total quality control and Deming's theory of management. *The American Statistician, 48*(3), 197–203.

Shewart, W. A. (1939). *Statistical method from the viewpoint of quality control.* Washington: The Graduate School the Department of Agriculture.

Chapter 8
Business Process Reengineering

BPR leads to deep redesign of business processes. It was popular during the 1990s basically as a reaction to recession; in those years companies needed to downsize and to better apply IT (Davenport and Short 1990; Cole 1994; Mumford 1994). In reviewing the literature it can be observed how the number of dedicated papers has decreased during the past 5 years. Hammer and Champy (1993) can be considered 'the parents' of BPR developing the first complete pattern to implement BPR.

According to Knights and Willmott (2000), BPR in the Plan stage improves cost, quality, service, speed and organisational transformation around processes. The approach to change is very fast and can be considered 'revolutionary'. Senior management should act an aggressive and autocratic style of leadership and employees become important only at a later stage. Consequently, BPR is more top-down or imposed than the other systems.

According to Hammer and Champy (1993), human resources involvement is important as well as teamwork, empowerment and responsibility. Limerick and Cunnington (1995) also argued that the strength of BPR lies in the empowerment of the individual. However, redistribution of responsibilities is an inevitable outcome of process reengineering (Davenport 1993) and this could lead to a 'hypermodern neo-authoritarianism' as Willmott suggested (1995). Knights and Willmott (2000), as already seen, claimed that BPR is mainly a top-down implementation and employees become important in the later stages. According to Hammer and Champy (1993) and Bradley (1994), similar to Six Sigma, there are precise players such as a steering committee; the 'czar', who ensures resources and knowledge for the projects; project leaders; process owners and reengineering teams.

In the Do stage, BPR is focused on the voice of the customer (Hammer and Champy 1993) and its capture. In addition, BPR is 'IT-minded', the reengineering cannot be carried out without using computers, software and databases. According to Kettinger et al. (1997), BPR techniques and tools are strongly based on mapping, benchmarking and IT; they include project management, brainstorming, cause-effect diagrams and problem solving (Klein 1994; Kettinger et al. 1997; Chou and Chou 2007).

A. Chiarini, *From Total Quality Control to Lean Six Sigma*, SpringerBriefs in Business,
DOI: 10.1007/978-88-470-2658-2_8,

The way of implementing BPR into the processes is underpinned by a well-structured pattern. Muthu et al. (1999) tried to summarise this approach for BPR. It is the sum of BPR methodologies described in the literature and it introduces five interesting steps similar to the PDCA cycle:

- preparing for BPR;
- map and analyse As-Is process;
- Design to-Be process;
- implementing reengineered processes;
- improving continuously.

Thyagarajan and Khatibi (2004, p. 58), tried to summarise the critical implementation factors discussed depicting reengineering in seven important areas:

- emphasise customer satisfaction;
- use performance improvement programmes and problem-solving techniques;
- focus on business processes;
- use teams and teamwork;
- bring about changes in values and beliefs;
- work to drive decision making down to lower levels in the organisation;
- require senior level commitment and change management for success.

References

Bradley, S. (1994). *Creating and adhering to a BPR methodology*. Gartner Group Report, pp. 1–30.

Chou, A. Y., & Chou, D. C. (2007). The complementary role of business process reengineering and information technology to total quality management practices. *International Journal of Information Systems and Change Management, 2*(1), 21–29.

Cole, R. (1994). Reengineering the corporation: A review essay. *Quality Management Journal, 1*(4), 77–85.

Davenport, T. H. (1993). *Process innovation: Re-engineering work through information technology*. Boston, MA: Harvard Business School Press.

Davenport, T. H., & Short, J. E. (1990). The new industrial engineering: Information technology and business process redesign. *Sloan Management Review, 31*(4), 11–27.

Hammer, M., & Champy, J. (1993). *Re-engineering the corporation: A manifesto for business revolution*. New York: Harper Business.

Kettinger, W. J., Teng, J. T. C., & Guha, S. (1997). Business process change: A study of methodologies, techniques, and tools. *MIS Quarterly, 21*(1), 55–80.

Klein, M. M. (1994). Reengineering methodologies and tools. A prescription for enhancing success. *Information Systems Management, 11*(2), 30–35.

Knights, D., & Wilmott, H. (2000). *The reengineering revolution?: Critical studies of corporate change*. London, UK: Sage.

Limerick, D., & Cunnington, B. (1995). *Managing the new organization: A blueprint for networks and strategic alliances*. Sydney, Australia: Business and Professional Publishing.

Mumford, E. (1994). New treatments or old remedies: Is business process reengineering really socio-technical design? *Journal of Strategic Information Systems, 3*(4), 313–326.

Muthu, S., Whitman, L. & Hossein, S. C. (1999). *Business process reengineering: A consolidated methodology*. Proceedings of the 4th Annual International Conference on Industrial Engineering Theory, Applications, and Practice. Department of the Interior Enterprise Architecture, U.S.

Thyagarajan, V., & Khatibi, A. (2004). BPR: A tool for managing the change. *Journal of Human Ecology, 15*(1), 57–61.

Willmott, H. (1995). The odd couple?: Re-engineering business processes; managing human relations. *New Technology, Work and Employment, 10*(2), 89–98.

Chapter 9
Lean Thinking

As seen in Chap. 2, since the 1970s competition has been increasing on factors such as zero defects, on-time delivery, price and relevant customisation (Piercy and Morgan 1997). This scenario is the opposite of the so-called 'Mass production' (Shingo 1989), in which there is a huge demand for products and services that are manufactured with low-cost resources and with poor personalisation and quality. In order to reduce the wastes that increase process lead time and reduce value added for the customers, Taiichi Ohno, past Toyota Production manager and Executive Vice President, invented TPS in the 1960s (Ohno 1988). Toyota has been focusing its efforts on reducing wastes within their manufacturing processes and increasing value added inside all the flow from suppliers to customers. Ohno (1988) identified seven types of manufacturing waste in order to improve processes and 'speed the flow':

- overproduction;
- inventory;
- extra processing steps;
- motion;
- defects;
- waiting;
- transportation.

Lean Production is a name derived from the book The Machine That Changed the World: The Story of Lean Production (Womack et al. 1991). Although Lean Production is focused on effectiveness in the production process, Lean Thinking is more focused on the efficiency in the company as a whole, including offices (Chiarini 2011).

In general, the shorter the process, the Leaner the organisation and consequently the fewer the wastes (Sugimori et al. 1977), thus Lean Thinking is focused on the extreme simplification of the 'mainstream' with the intent of avoiding any kind of waste and accelerating the flow.

In the Plan stage the typical system for deploying strategies is hoshin kanri, introduced at the same time for JTQC (King 1989). The typical goals to follow are

A. Chiarini, *From Total Quality Control to Lean Six Sigma*, SpringerBriefs in Business,
DOI: 10.1007/978-88-470-2658-2_9, © The Author(s) 2012

linked to waste reduction, as well as COPQ and customer satisfaction (George 2002). Over time Lean has proposed interesting new metrics along with its typical tools, such as lead time and Overall Equipment Effectiveness (OEE) (Nakajima 1988) to mention a few.

Lean Thinking is for long-term oriented managers with a very clear vision (Womack and Jones 1998). Managers are bound to create a culture of getting quality right the first time similar to TQC and TQM, going and seeing for themselves problems and improvements in the processes (Liker 2004).

According to Womack et al. (1991), quick and voluntary teams continually try to remove wastes and there is not a pattern as rigorous and hierarchical as the Define, Measure, Analyse, Improve and Control (DMAIC) of Six Sigma for improvement projects. Only through reviewing practitioner literature or by directly analysing case studies, can it be found that teams usually manage 'Kaizen events' or 'Kaizen weeks' (Robertson et al. 1992; Manos and Alukal 2006; Manos 2007; Dickson et al. 2009), where Kaizen is the Japanese translation of continuous improvement. The peculiarity of these improvement projects is the short duration (on average a week) and the maximum involvement of people (Wickens 1993; Liker and Meier 2006). Similarly to JTQC, all the employees at all levels should be involved, creating an atmosphere of continuous learning and respect for people (Liker 2004). Ohno (1988), who is considered one of the fathers of Lean, proposed in his book the same JTQC concept of respect for humanity presented by Ishikawa (1985).

The Do stage is particularly characterised by specific tools such as 5S, Kanban, Heijunka, Total Productive Maintenance and many others (Nakajima 1988; Ohno 1988; Shingo 1989) invented by Toyota and other Japanese companies. Lean does not need advanced statistical training, nor certified Black and Green Belts. Self-empowerment and responsibility are as important as team building and team efforts. There is no trace in the academic literature of the application of Lean Tools in engineering departments. Companies prefer tools derived from TQC–TQM and Six Sigma that are specialised for engineering and design. There is not, for instance, an approach similar to the so-called Design for Six Sigma (DFSS) (Coronado and Antony 2002; Yang and El-Haik 2009).

The hoshin kanri drives a strategic process of review (Witcher and Butterworth 2001) in the Check and Act stages, and day-by-day results are managed by visual control (Shingo 1989). This peculiar tool has led to the principles that no problems have to be hidden, that production can be stopped to fix them and last, but not least, people can learn from mistakes (Liker 2004). Similarly to Deming, some authors linked to the Lean Accounting topic (Maskell and Baggaley 2004; Kennedy and Widener 2008) discussed how to fix standards and targets for cost, but indicators can be dangerous to the continuous improvement principle.

9.1 Lean Principles and Tools

Although it is not the main purpose of this book to take account of Lean principles and tools, the following paragraphs introduce them and their goals to aid readers' understanding. Lean has many tools and principles; the book explains the most used inside the companies. Pavnaskar et al. (2003) wrote a paper dedicated to a complete classification of Lean tools and matching them with their associated type of waste.

9.1.1 Hoshin Kanri and Planning

Lean Thinking has to be linked to strategic objectives. Senior management usually deploys strategic objectives in the processes using particular systems such as Balanced Scorecard (Kaplan and Norton 1996) and Hoshin Kanri (Witcher and Butterworth 2001). Balanced Scorecard is the classic deployment approach invented at Harvard Business School in the 1990s by Kaplan and norton, whereas Hoshin Kanri is a pure Japanese system. This latter was developed in the 1960s at Bridgestone Japan and then theorised for the first time by Miyaji (Miyaji 1969 quoted by Kondo 1998). Through particular matrixes structured in four quadrants, strategies are typically first deployed in tactics or action plans, then in processes and lastly in results (Jackson 2006; Cudney 2009).

9.1.2 Value Stream Mapping

Value Stream Mapping (VSM) is the first tool used to see within the processes. Material flows and information flows that control the material are mapped by VSM. This visual representation boosts the process of Lean implementation by helping to identify the value-adding and non-value adding activities.

VSM comprises two maps: the Current State and the Future State Map. VSM uses standardised symbols for mapping the process and follows the entire flow of a product, service or product family from the suppliers to the customers.

9.1.3 Lean Office

Wastes are not found just in the production processes. The seven wastes principle can also be applied to administration, support, marketing and other office processes. These latter are normally mapped and improved after applying Lean tools in the shop floor (Huls 2005). Applying Lean to the office processes is different from production because within the office there are transactions instead of products, sometimes these are not easily visible (Subramoniam 2009). For instance, the wastes could be a backlog of electronic orders, long approval processes, documents waiting to be signed and so on (Keyte and Locher 2004).

9.1.4 Lean Metrics

The results of waste reduction are measured by efficiency and effectiveness indicators. Lean has many indicators; among the most important metrics are lead-time, on-time delivery, overall equipment effectiveness, process cycle efficiency, process cycle time, work-in-process (WIP), throughput rate and many others. Through Hoshin Kanri, strategic objectives are usually linked to Lean Key Performance Indicators. Indicators should be measured and managed inside the processes day-by-day or even day-by-the hour (Maskell and Baggaley 2004).

9.1.5 Push and Pull Systems

Push and Pull are completely different ways of manufacturing. Push is based on forecasts of sales and thus the organisation manufactures pushing the products into the warehouses (Make To Stock). Pull, the opposite, is when production is launched and pulled only by orders (Make To Order). Pull is the typical system used in mass production where the product demand is stable and predictable, few products are personalised and the warehouse cost is not high.

9.1.6 Kaizen Event

Continuous improvement is the English translation of the Japanese term Kaizen, a principle made known by Masaaki's book Kaizen (Masaaki 1986). The Kaizen Event is a quick and full-immersion event for solving a problem or reducing waste; it takes from 2 to 5 days and it is carried out by personnel at all levels using the tools and principles described in the next paragraphs.

9.1.7 Visual Control and Management

Workers and managers have to control and visualize immediately the waste at the shop floor. This means that all the shop-floor indicators and problems have to be controlled and managed by the means of displays, signals, horns and other systems in real time.

9.1.8 Takt Time

Takt time is a German term that derives from the 'Produktionstak' system applied at Focke-Wulff aircraft works in Germany (Holweg 2006). In brief, it is the rhythm of the sales or frequency at which the customer needs the product. It affects all the processes from sales to the suppliers because it sets the rhythm at which the product and its components should be made. A faster production could introduce inventories and a slower production could delay the delivery.

9.1.9 5s

The 5S are 5 precise steps for setting in order and having an area cleaned up. A messy workplace, desk or manufacturing area makes it hard to find things, easier to get distracted, and can introduce accidents, mistakes and lower productivity (Pavnaskars et al. 2003). The five steps are: Sort, sort needed and unneeded items; Set in Order, arrange things in their proper place; Shine, clean up the workplace; Standardize, standardize the first three S's method; and Sustain, make 5S a part of your duty. 5S is one the most visual Lean tools.

9.1.10 One-Piece-Flow

The shortening of product/service life cycles and the increasing demands for customisation make it difficult to produce the products on traditional production lines structured for relevant quantities (Miltenburg 2001). Using one-piece-flow, traditional lines are replaced by a U-shaped cell in which there is every activity and all equipment useful for the product/service. Cells can be dedicated either to a single product, when it has high volumes, or to several products through a mixed-model concept. When using the one-piece-flow tool it becomes fundamental to change quickly from one part-number product to the next.

9.1.11 SMED: Quick Changeover

Quick Changeover, also known in the manufacturing field as SMED (Single Minute Exchange of Die), is a particular tool that avoids dead times and reduces the set-up operations; it was developed for the first time inside Toyota by Shigeo Shingo in 1955 (Shingo 1986). The reduction in set-up times means that workers can change part-numbers that go over the machine more frequently and consequently reduce WIP inventories.

9.1.12 Jidoka: Autonomation

Jidoka is an automatic system that checks machine or product characteristics and stops production in the case of nonconformity. It does not require worker control. Jidoka has the same principle of Poka-Yoke or Mistake Proofing tools for avoiding, not necessarily in an automatic way, human errors on the processes to reduce defects.

9.1.13 Kanban

Kanban consists of two Japanese words: 'kan' that means visual, and 'ban' that means card or board; it was introduced for the first time by Ohno in 1956 in Toyota. Kanban works like supermarket shelves: in a supermarket the customer can get what is needed at the time needed in the amount needed. The supermarket only stocks what it can sell and the customers only take what they need because future supply is assured. In the same way a production line or cell has 'supermarket shelves' in which there is the right quantity of products that has to be worked. The rate of this replenishment is controlled by a kanban card system that gives permission to produce to the cell or line to assure supply (Sugimori et al. 1977). In this way kanban levels off the flow reducing the WIP and introducing the so-called just-in-time.

9.1.14 Total Productive Maintenance

Total Productive Maintenance (TPM) is a fundamental pillar of Lean, a mandatory system for introducing preventive maintenance of the machines, equipment and raising the awareness of the workers about self-maintenance. Nakajima (1988) wrote an interesting book in which TPM is presented as the combination of two parts: the preventive maintenance and the total involvement of workers. The first part, based on a statistical approach, derived from US engineering research, whereas the second is the typical Japanese approach. TPM, when well applied, reduces machine down-time, as well as product defects.

9.1.15 Asaichi: Market Morning: A3 Report

Masaaki (1997) explained how workers and engineers have to solve problems as soon as possible directly in the 'Gemba' (Japanese translation of manufacturing floor). The Asaichi morning market is the Japanese market where fish, fruits and vegetables are prepared and sold in the early morning when they are fresh. In the same way, every morning a team controls and reviews the 'fresh' nonconformities of the last day using a quick problem-solving method registered and displayed in an A3 report.

References

Chiarini, A. (2011). Integrating lean thinking into ISO 9001: A first guideline. *International Journal of Lean Six Sigma, 2*(2), 96–117.

Coronado, R. B., & Antony, J. (2002). Critical success factors for the successful implementation of six sigma projects in organizations. *The TQM Magazine, 14*(2), 92–99.

Cudney, E. (2009). *Using hoshin kanri to improve the value stream.* London, UK: Taylor and Francis.

Dickson, E. W., Singh, S., Cheung, S. C., Wyatt, C. C., & Nugent, A. S. (2009). Application of lean manufacturing techniques in the emergency department. *The Journal of Emergency Medicine, 37*(2), 177–182.

George, M. (2002). *Lean six sigma: Combining six sigma quality with lean production speed.* New York: McGraw-Hill.

Holweg, M. (2006). The genealogy of lean production. *Journal of Operations Management, 25*(2), 420–437.

Huls, K. (2005). The antioch company brings lean into the office. *Journal of Organizational Excellence, 24*(4), 31–38.

Ishikawa, K. (1985). *What is total quality control? The Japanese way.* Englewood Cliffs, NJ: Prentice-Hall.

Jackson, T. L. (2006). *Hoshin kanri for the lean enterprise: Developing competitive capabilities and managing profit.* New York: Productivity Press.

Kaplan, R. S., & Norton, D. P. (1996). Using the balanced scorecard as a strategic management system. *Harvard Business Review, Best of HBR*, 1–14.

Kennedy, F. A., & Widener, S. K. (2008). A control framework: Insight from evidence on lean accounting. *Management Accounting Research, 19*(4), 301–323.

Keyte, B., & Locher, D. (2004). *The complete lean enterprise: Value stream mapping for administrative and office processes.* New York: Productivity Press.

King, R. (1989). *Hoshin planning: The development approach.* MA: GOAL/QPC, Methuen.

Kondo, Y. (1998). Hoshin kanri—a participative way of quality management in Japan. *The TQM Magazine, 10*(6), 425–431.

Liker, J. K. (2004). *The Toyota way—14 management principles from the world's greatest manufacturer.* New York: McGraw-Hill.

Liker, J. K., & Meier, D. (2006). Automation, motivation and lean production reconsidered. *Assembly Automation, 26*(2), 98–103.

Manos, A. (2007). The benefits of kaizen and kaizen events. Quality progress. http://www.proferoinc.com/pdf/qp0207lean.pdf. Retrieved from Mar 2010.

Manos, A., & Alukal, G. (2006). *Lean kaizen.* Milwaukee, WI: Quality Press.

Masaaki, I. (1986). *Kaizen: The key to Japan's competitive success.* New York: McGraw-Hill.

Masaaki, I. (1997). *Gemba kaizen, a commonsense, low-cost approach to management*. New York: McGraw-Hill.

Maskell, B. H., & Baggaley, B. (2004). *Practical lean accounting: A proven system for measuring and managing the lean enterprise*. New York: Productivity Press.

Miltenburg, J. (2001). One-piece flow manufacturing on U-shaped production lines: A tutorial. *IIE Transactions, 33*(4), 303–321.

Nakajima, S. (1988). *Introduction to TPM: Total productive maintenance*. Cambridge, MA: Productivity Press.

Ohno, T. (1988). *Toyota production system: Beyond large scale production*. Cambridge, MA: Productivity Press.

Pavnaskar, S. J., Gershenson, J. K., & Jambekar, A. B. (2003). Classification scheme for lean manufacturing tools. *International Journal of Production Research, 41*(13), 3075–3090.

Piercy, N. F., & Morgan, N. A. (1997). The impact of lean thinking and the lean enterprise on marketing: Threat or synergy? *Journal of Marketing Management, 13*(7), 679–693.

Robertson, D., Rinehart, J., & Huxley, C. (1992). Team concept and kaizen: Japanese production management in a unionized canadian auto plant. *Studies in Political Economy, 39*(4), 77–107.

Shingo, S. (1986). *Zero quality control: Source inspection and the poka-yoke system study*. Cambridge, MA: Productivity Press.

Shingo, S. (1989). *A study of the Toyota production system from an industrial engineering viewpoint*. Cambridge, MA: Productivity Press.

Subramoniam, R., Abusamra, G., & Hostetler, D. (2009). *Lean engineering implementation challenges for automotive remanufacturing*, Paper presented at SAE world congress and exhibition, session: Lean and six sigma: Getting the most out of your quality toolbox. April 2009, Detroit, MI, available at (not freely available). http://papers.sae.org/2009-01-1188. Retrieved from 10 Dec 2010.

Sugimori, Y., Kusunoki, K., Cho, F., & Uchikawa, S. (1977). Toyota production system and kanban system: Materialization of just-in-time and respect-for-human system. *International Journal of Production Research, 15*(6), 553–564.

Wickens, P. D. (1993). Lean production and beyond: The system, its critics and the future. *Human Resource Management Journal, 3*(4), 75–90.

Witcher, B. J., & Butterworth, R. (2001). Hoshin kanri: Policy management in Japanese-owned UK subsidiaries. *Journal of Management Studies, 38*(5), 651–674.

Womack, J. P., & Jones, D. T. (1998). *Lean thinking: Banish waste and create wealth in your corporation*. New York: Simon & Schuster.

Womack, J. P., Jones, D. T., & Ross, D. (1991). *The machine that changed the world: The story of lean production*. New York: Harper Collins.

Yang, K., & El-Haik, B. (2009). *Design for six sigma: A roadmap for product*. New York: McGraw-Hill.

Chapter 10
Six Sigma

Six Sigma as a measurement standard in product variation can be traced back to the 1930s when Walter Shewart (1939) showed the correlation between levels of sigma from the mean and the defects produced in a process. When a range around a defined target is fixed it can be statistically demonstrated that the more the number of sigma stays inside the range, the less the probability that the outcome is a failure. Failure means that the outcome is outside the range and consequently the products or services are defective. Many measurement standards entered the scientific and management literature later but the term 'Six Sigma' was coined by a Motorola engineer named Bill Smith. Motorola is an American multinational telecommunications company based in Schaumburg, Illinois, which was divided in 2009 into two independent public companies.

In the early and mid-1980s with Chairman Bob Galvin, Motorola engineers decided that the traditional quality levels that measured defects in thousands of opportunities did not provide enough quality results; instead, they wanted to measure the defects per million opportunities (DPMO). Motorola developed the new Six Sigma standard, created the methodology and the required cultural change associated with it. Six Sigma helped Motorola realise powerful bottom-line results in the entire organisation; in fact, Motorola documented more than $16 billion in savings because of Six Sigma efforts. Since then, hundreds of companies around the world have adopted Six Sigma as a way of doing business. This is a direct result of many of USA's leaders openly praising the benefits of Six Sigma: leaders such as Larry Bossidy of Allied Signal (now Honeywell) and Jack Welch of General Electric Company (Harry and Schroeder 2000).

10.1 Six Sigma as an Excellence Management System

Six Sigma is a management system similar to TQM, BPR or Lean Thinking. It is considered a system for reaching business excellence (Klefsjo et al. 2001; Adebanjo 2001) and it focuses on a precise application pattern called DMAIC

A. Chiarini, *From Total Quality Control to Lean Six Sigma*, SpringerBriefs in Business,
DOI: 10.1007/978-88-470-2658-2_10,

Table 10.1 Correlation among sigma of a process, DPMO and CPQ (from Harry and Schroeder 2000)

Sigma level	DPMO (Defects Per Million Opportunities)	CPQ (Cost of Poor Quality)
2	308.537	Not applicable
3	66.807	25–40 % of turnover
4	6210 (typical company)	15–25 % of turnover
5	233	5–15 % of turnover
6	3, 4	<1 % of turnover

(Klefsjo et al. 2001). It improves customer satisfaction along with all organisational performance (Przekop 2003). The main worldwide companies use Six Sigma, especially those quoted in Wall Street (Pande et al. 2000; Senapati 2004).

After Motorola, other important companies such as GE, Allied Signal, Caterpillar and many others chose Six Sigma and obtained significant savings in terms of 'Cost Of Poor Quality' (COPQ).

Some authors (e.g. McAuley et al. 2007) dealt with neo-modernist organisation theory, introducing the 'new-wave management'.

These authors see Six Sigma and other similar management systems from a highly critical perspective. Six Sigma can impose onto organisations increased levels of control that deny the possibility of autonomy and professional independence.

10.2 Six Sigma Model

Since the late 1990s innumerable articles have been written on Six Sigma. Harry and Schroeder's (2000) model is now hailed as the classical Six Sigma model for the manufacturing sector. The first author, in particular, as an ex-Motorola manager, has been able to analyse the model directly in the organisation that conceived it, and used it better. In their book, 'Six Sigma: The Breakthrough Management Strategy Revolutionizing the World's Top Corporations', Harry and Schroeder delineate the basic model that is used today, substantially, in all manufacturing and service organisations.

In an approximate way, the authors puts in correlation the sigma level of a process (any process, from marketing to customer care) with the number of defects and the CPQ to which the organisation is subjected, as shown in Table 10.1.

This table is very important in the Six Sigma model because it 'certifies' the achievement of a determined level of sigma both on a specific project and process, up to the whole organisation. Continually obtaining higher levels of sigma, the organisation numerically shows the reduction in the CPQ and obtains a precise saving.

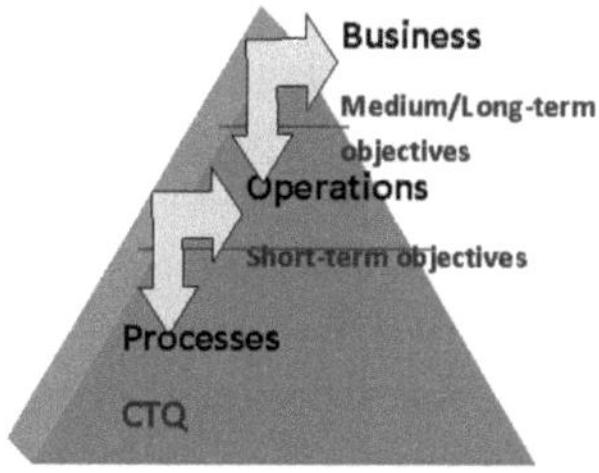

Fig. 10.1 The deployment from the business plan

10.2.1 The Six Sigma DMAIC Pattern

In the classical approach there are five stages for the realisation of strategic projects in Six Sigma and they are known as the acronym DMAIC (Pande et al. 2000; Breyfogle 2003; Pyzdek 2009):

- D—Define;
- M—Measure;
- A—Analyse;
- I—Improve;
- C—Control.

It is not difficult to connect the five phases of DMAIC with Deming's (1982) classical approach: Plan—Do—Check—Act (PDCA). According to Harry and Schroeder (2000), the five stages are applicable to different levels of the organisation:

- business;
- operations;
- process.

In fact, every stage of DMAIC represents the deployment of the precedent according to the classical management system deployment (Kaplan and Norton 1996). The D of DMAIC, for instance, expects the definition of long-and medium-term objectives from the business level in a Business Plan. The medium-and long-term objectives are turned into a definition of objectives of a brief period (one year) for the operations level. The objectives of the brief period also define the CTQ of the processes connected to the attainment of the objectives as shown in Fig. 10.1. This strict link between strategies and CTQs is one of the changes introduced by Six Sigma.

At the process level, the Six Sigma DMAIC methodology can be thought of as a path for problem solving and continuous improvement. Most companies begin implementing Six Sigma using the DMAIC methodology, and later add the Design for Six Sigma (DFSS) methodology when the organisational culture and experience level allows projects to be conducted in the technical departments.

For each phase, a team formed by a Black Belt and several Green Belts uses classical tools derived from the quality world. Many authors, especially consultants, list these tools that are by now well established for manufacturing (Pande et al. 2000; Breyfogle 2003; Pyzdek 2009; George 2002).

Table 10.2 synthesises the tools used in the classical model in correspondence to the DMAIC stages. It can be noted that Six Sigma did not invent any new tools rather Six Sigma just better arranged the tools derived from TQM and Lean Thinking.

Table 10.2 shows, in a precise way, how a project of improvement that follows the DMAIC stages needs knowledge of advanced statistic tools such as Anova and Design Of Experiments (DOE). The projects, because of their nature, involve a team for a period varying from a few months up to one year, or even more, according to the typology of saving required.

The power of the Six Sigma DMAIC pattern lies in the structure and the rigour of the approach. Of the hundreds of quality and organisational tools that have been developed over the years, the specific team of Black Belts and Green Belts uses the most important tools for the kind of project.

10.2.2 The Roles in Six Sigma

The players traditionally involved in Six Sigma projects are described below (Brue 2000; Pande et al. 2000; Snee and Hoerl 2003).

- Senior Champion or Sponsor (Executive Leader):

He or she is the CEO or the Head of Office that decides to introduce the strategic model Six Sigma. The Senior Champion appoints one or more:

- Champions:

Champions, together with the Senior Champion, decide the projects and the strategic objectives on which Six Sigma is applied. The Champion appoints the:

- Master Black Belt:

This is a manager or a consultant that manages the training and works as 'coach' on the Six Sigma projects. The principal assignment is to ensure that the whole organisation receives the appropriate knowledge on the methods and tools. The Master Black Belt and the Black Belt decide the projects and the processes on which to operate that are connected to the objectives decided by the Champion.

- Black Belt:

The Black Belts are team leaders on specific projects and they manage all he resources and the necessary knowledge for the project. They have, naturally, to know the tools of quality and problem solving well, as well as project management and team building. Every Black Belt manages a team composed of:

- Green Belts:

They are the operative components of the team devoted to a specific project. Their principal assignment is to follow, day by day, the project and the measures. They have less detailed knowledge of the tools for quality. In the USA and Europe,

Table 10.2 DMAIC and tools used in the manufacturing sector

DMAIC Phase steps	Tools used
D—Define Phase: Define the project goals and customer (internal and external) needs.	
• Define customers and requirements (CTQs)	• Project charter
• Develop problem statement, goals and benefits	• Process flowchart
• Identify champion, process owner and team	• SIPOC diagram
• Define resources	• Stakeholder analysis
• Evaluate key organizational support	• CTQ matrix definition
• Develop project plan and milestones	• Quality function deployment (QFD)—kano analysis
• Develop high level process map	
Define tollgate review	
M—Measure phase: Measure the process to determine current performance; quantify the problem.	
• Define defect, opportunity, unit and metrics	
• Detailed process map of appropriate areas	• Data collection plan/example
• Develop data collection plan	• Benchmarking
• Validate the measurement system	• Measurement system analysis/gage R&R
• Collect the data	
• Begin developing Y = f(x) relationship	• Voice of the customer gathering
• Determine process C pability and sigma baseline	• Cp, Cp
Measure tollgate review	
A—Analyse phase: Analyse and determine the root cause(s) of the defects.	
• Define performance objectives	• Histogram
• Identify value/non-value added process steps	• Pareto chart
• Identify sources of variation	• Time series/run chart
• Determine root cause(s)	• Scatter plot
• Determine vital few x's, Y = f(x) relationship	• Regression analysis
	• Cause and effect/fishbone diagram
	• 5 whys
	• Process map review and analysis
	• Statistical analysis
	• Hypothesis testing (continuous and discrete)
	• Non-normal data analysis
Analyse tollgate review	
I—Improve Phase: Improve the process by eliminating defects.	
• Perform design of experiments	• Brainstorming
• Develop potential solutions	• Mistake proofing
• Define operating tolerances of potential system	• Design of experiments
• Assess failure modes of potential solutions	• Failure modes and effects analysis—FMEA
• Validate potential improvement by pilot studies	• Simulation software
• Correct/re-evaluate potential solution	

(continued)

Table 10.2 (continued)

DMAIC Phase steps	Tools used
Improve tollgate review	
C—Control Phase: Control future process performance.	
• Define and validate monitoring and control system	• Process sigma calculation, Cp–Cpk
• Develop standards and procedures	• Control charts (variable and attribute)
• Implement statistical process control	
• Determine process capability	• Cost savings calculations
• Develop transfer plan, handoff to process owner	• Control plan
• Verify benefits, cost savings/avoidance, profit growth	
• Close project, finalize documentation	
• Commun cate to business, celebrate	
Control tollgate review	

Table 10.3 Six sigma training certification

Role	Training
Black belt (BB)	Four weeks of training (one week/month)
	A week of statistics of base, seven tools and analysis of the data
	A week of DOE, FMEA, QFD
	A week of advanced statistic control for quality
	A week of project management, management and team motivation
	Project six sigma to be brought ahead with a MBB and one autonomously
Master black belt (MBB)	Certified following 20 projects with success as BB

different organisations have adopted a consolidated scheme for the certification of the Black Belt and Master Black Belt as summarised in Table 10.3.

10.3 Six Sigma and PDCA

Six Sigma is a long-term journey. According to Harry and Schroeder (2000), Six Sigma has a specific deployment starting from the Business Plan. Harry (1998) and Harry and Schroeder (2000) claim that Six Sigma leads mainly to reduction of poor quality cost; this point can also be found in the work of several other authors (Coronado and Antony 2002; Wiper and Harrison 2000; Antony and Banuelas 2002; Antony 2004).

The DPMO concept is not just a slogan but a very grounded way to measure how successfully Six Sigma objectives are implemented. It has been demonstrated 'on the field' that Six Sigma improves business performance in many ways and, in the final analysis, company margins (Harry 1998; Slater 1999). Some authors

(Davison and Al-Shaghana 2007) have pointed out how Six Sigma organisations have a higher quality culture than non-Six Sigma organisations and managers have a clear quality vision.

Six Sigma is not focused on social responsibility results (Goh 2002), even though some authors (Kuei and Madu 2003) believe that with some limits Six Sigma needs to extend to include environmental management and safety dimensions.

Six Sigma projects take on average from a few months (Goh 2002) to one year and thus their yield is short-to medium-term based.

Reviewing the literature concerning the management of the organisation, many authors deal with two important figures: top and senior managers and their commitment to an effective and long-lasting Six Sigma application (Harry and Schroeder 2000; Henderson and Evans Henderson and Evans 2000; Coronado and Antony 2002; Antony and Banuelas 2002; Linderman et al. 2003).

A 'sponsor' and a 'champion' are supposed to manage the company as a whole towards Six Sigma. Hence, without a clear and well-noticed top management commitment Six Sigma can fail after a few months of implementation. In addition, leadership and strategic management for Six Sigma should be 'visionary' because culture and charisma can easily move strategies to processes.

Starting from the paper of Harry (1998), it is taken for granted that Six Sigma organisation needs important figures such as Master Black Belt, Black Belt and Green Belt. Black and Green Belts should be certified through precise and well-coded training (Harry and Schroeder 2000). A Master Black Belt usually is a Black Belt who has successfully carried out several projects and can act as a trainer for Black and Green Belts.

Six Sigma teams led by a Black or Green Belt need worker participation as well. Linderman et al. (2003) dealt with the aspect that Six Sigma organisations should, by extensive programmes, train all the employees. Therefore, at this level, Six Sigma requires team building and team efforts and each Six Sigma team leader is supposed to be trained on these subjects not only on statistics. However, Hahn et al. (2000), in their discussion about statistics training, referred to a 'democratisation of statistics' within Six Sigma. Every employee should be trained, at the requested level for his/her role, on statistics and quality tools. Six Sigma programmes have to balance the cultural and technical skills (Eckes 2001) of every worker. In this way Six Sigma introduces a hierarchical participation of staff in decision making and a precise development of the skills which employees are bound to acquire. Managers should select the best employees for projects (Brue 2000) based on their abilities to bring assigned tasks to a close. Each participant within Six Sigma projects is controlled by a Black or Green Belt but participants are supposed to take on responsibility about rules and scheduling. It is not so difficult to notice how employees are led and managed mainly by extrinsic motivations, rather than intrinsic ones.

The role of employees within the improvement team has received some criticism in terms of commitment and motivation. Goh (2002), for instance, analysed Six Sigma limits, pointed out that it hardly sustains creativity, breakthrough or

Table 10.4 Six sigma versus lean organization

	Six sigma	Lean organization
Focus	Variation reduction	Waste reduction
Improvement projects	DMAIC pattern use of certified black and green belts certified savings	Value stream mapping kaizen week, quick and operative improvement and maximum involvement first of all
Tools and techniques	Quality and problem solving tools, project management	Toyota production system tools

entrepreneurship among staff. The author in his findings stated that Six Sigma is not suitable for enhancing creativity and ability of interpretation as well as priorities of the organisation, especially economical, and it can sacrifice growth of people and talent development. Therefore extrinsic motivations in terms of customer satisfaction and savings are more important than intrinsic motivations such as growth of staff.

In the Do stage it is fundamental to capture the voice of the customer. Six Sigma tends to cut down external COPQ (Harrington 1986) such as warranty costs, returned goods and penalties. According to El-Haik and Al-Aomar (2006) and Pyzdek (2009), this is what Six Sigma does better, especially through Quality Function Deployment, a tool used in the first stages of the project.

According to Byrne and Norris (2003), the DMAIC pattern is perhaps the most important part of Six Sigma DNA. DMAIC is something unique and it helps in the deployment of projects without failures; every stage, from Define to Control, is validated through a 'tollgate' check, which can stop the project if the result stage is not what is expected. Design processes are instead well managed using the DFSS pattern (Coronado and Antony 2002; Yang and El-Haik 2009).

Within the DMAIC pattern, Six Sigma teams can use numerous tools dependent on the scope and the kind of stage. Among these, Six Sigma inherits well-known quality management tools (Klefsjo et al. 2001; Dahlgaard and Dahlgaard-Park 2006), including advanced statistical tools. Six Sigma has also borrowed tools derived from TPS (George 2002, 2003; Bendell 2006). The DMAIC toolset is very open and can be surely enlarged in the future.

Six Sigma has a strong approach based on facts and data. All the project results are validated using 'sigma level' around the target. In several companies, the finance department is assigned to calculate and report these savings to senior management. The results of the project can be submitted to an actual external certification (Pyzdek 2009) led by auditors. Hahn et al. (2000) are convinced that the disciplined data-driven approach is the foundation of Six Sigma.

The results of each Six Sigma project should be collected in order to learn from them. In this way, companies like GE are using a database for the projects and their features (Slater 1999) as well as statistics software. Snee and Horler (2003) pointed out that many companies celebrate the Six Sigma teams and spread Six Sigma results to all the staff; Harry and Schoereder (2000) suggested a specific communication plan to reach this goal.

In the first years of 2000 Six Sigma encountered Lean Thinking (George 2002; Smith 2003) creating 'Lean Six Sigma'. Nowadays it is considered a well-established system for process improvement as confirmed by several authors (Arnheiter and Maleyeff 2005; Kumar et al. 2006; Wedgwood 2006). The marriage seems to be happy. Indeed Six Sigma is problem focused and it assumes that process variation is waste because it generates defects and COPQ. In addition to design processes, Six Sigma proposes the interesting DFSS system. Lean Thinking, by contrast, is focused on process flow and lead time and views any activity that does not add value as waste. Therefore it combines the 'speed' introduced by Lean, and Six Sigma capability of reducing variation. Nevertheless, in reviewing the authors above mentioned along with George (2002, 2003), Lean Six Sigma looks more like a DMAIC pattern enhanced with Lean tools than the real fusion of two systems. Table 10.4 summarises the main differences between the systems.

References

Adebanjo, D. (2001). TQM and business excellence: Is there really a conflict? *Measuring Business Excellence, 5*(3), 37–40.

Antony, J. (2004). Some pros and cons of six sigma: An academic perspective. *The TQM Magazine, 16*(4), 303–306.

Antony, J., & Banuelas, R. (2002). Key ingredients for the effective implementation of six sigma program. *Measuring Business Excellence, 6*(4), 20–27.

Arnheiter, E. D., & Maleyeff, J. (2005). The integration of lean management and six sigma. *The TQM Magazine, 17*(1), 5–18.

Bendell, T. (2006). A review and comparison of six sigma and the lean organizations. *The TQM Magazine, 18*(3), 255–262.

Breyfogle, F. W. (2003). *Implementing six sigma: Smarter solutions using statistical methods.* New York: John Wiley and Sons.

Brue, G. (2000). *Six sigma for team members.* Pagosa Springs, CO: Morningstar Communications Group.

Byrne, G., & Norris, B. (2003). Drive baldrige level performance. *Six Sigma Forum Magazine, 2*(3), 13–21.

Coronado, R. B., & Antony, J. (2002). Critical success factors for the successful implementation of six sigma projects in organizations. *The TQM Magazine, 14*(2), 92–99.

Dahlgaard, J. J., & Dahlgaard-Park, S. M. (2006). Lean production, six sigma quality, TQM and company culture. *The TQM Magazine, 18*(3), 263–281.

Davison, L., & Al-Shaghana, K. (2007). The link between six sigma and quality culture—An empirical study. *Total Quality Management & Business Excellence, 18*(3 and 4), 249–265.

Eckes, G. (2001). *Making six sigma last: Managing the balance between cultural and technical change.* New York: Wiley.

El-Haik, B., & Al-Aomar, R. (2006). *Simulation-based lean six-sigma and design for six-sigma.* Hoboken, NJ: Wiley.

George, M. (2002). *Lean six sigma: Combining six sigma quality with lean production speed.* New York: McGraw-Hill.

George, M. (2003). *Lean six sigma for service.* New York: McGraw-Hill.

Goh, T. N. (2002). A strategic assessment of six sigma. *Quality and Reliability Engineering International, 18*(5), 403–410.

Hahn, G. J., Doganaksoy, N., & Hoerl, R. (2000). The evolution of six sigma. *Quality Engineering, 12*(3), 317–326.

Harrington, H. J. (1986). *Poor-quality cost.* Milwaukee, WI: ASQ Quality Press.

Harry, M. J. (1998). Six sigma: A breakthrough strategy for profitability. *Quality Progress, 31*(5), 60–64.
Harry, M. J., & Schroeder, R. (2000). *The breakthrough management strategy revolutionizing the world's top corporations*. New York: Doubleday.
Henderson, K. M., & Evans, J. R. (2000). Successful implementation of six sigma: Benchmarking GE company. *Benchmarking: An International Journal, 7*(4), 260–281.
Kaplan, R. S., & Norton, D. P. (1996). Using the balanced scorecard as a strategic management system. *Harvard Business Review, Best of HBR*, pp. 1–14.
Klefsjo, B., Wiklund, H., & Edgeman, R. L. (2001). Six sigma seen as a methodology for total quality management. *Measuring Business Excellence, 5*(1), 31–35.
Kuei, C. H., & Madu, C. N. (2003). Customer-centric six sigma quality and reliability management. *International Journal of Quality & Reliability Management, 20*(8), 954–964.
Kumar, M., Antony, J., Singhc, R. K., Tiwarid, M. K., & Perry, D. (2006). Implementing the lean sigma framework in an Indian SME: A case study. *Production Planning & Control, 17*(4), 407–423.
Linderman, K., Schroeder, R. G., Zaheer, S., & Choo, A. S. (2003). Six sigma: A goaltheoretic perspective. *Journal of Operations Management, 3*(21), 193–203.
McAuley, J., Duberley, J., & Johnson, P. (2007). *Organization theory, challenges and perspectives*. London: Pearson Education Limited.
Pande, P. S., Neuman, R. P., & Cavanagh, R. R. (2000). *The six sigma way: How GE, Motorola and other top companies are honing their performance*. New York: McGraw-Hill Professional.
Przekop, P. (2003). *Six sigma for business excellence: A manager's guide to supervising six sigma projects and teams*. New York: McGraw-Hill.
Pyzdek, T. (2009). *The six sigma handbook: A complete guide for greenbelts, blackbelts, and managers at all levels*. New York: McGraw-Hill.
Senapati, N. R. (2004). Six sigma: Myths and realities. *International Journal of Quality & Reliability Management, 21*(6), 683–690.
Shewart, W. A. (1939). *Statistical methodfrom the viewpoint of quality control*. Washington, DC: The Graduate School the Department of Agriculture.
Slater, R. (1999). *Jack Welch and the GE way: Management insights and leadership secrets of the legendary CEO*. New York: McGraw-Hill.
Smith, B. (2003). Lean and six sigma-a one-two punch. *Quality Progress*. Retrieved from June 15, 2000 http://www.tbmcg.com/acrobat/press_public/QP_-_Lean_and_Six_Sigma_-_One_Two_Punch.pdf.
Snee, R. D., & Hoerl, R. W. (2003). *Leading six sigma*. Upper Saddle River, New York: Prentice-Hall.
Wedgwood, I. (2006). *Lean sigma, a practitioner's guide*. Upper Saddle River, NJ: Prentice Hall.
Wiper, B., & Harrison, A. (2000). Deployment of six sigma methodologies in human resource function: A case study. *Total Quality Management, 11*(4), 270–728.
Yang, K., & El-Haik, B. (2009). *Design for six sigma: A roadmap for product*. New York: McGraw-Hill.

Chapter 11
Discussion and Comparison About the Common Characteristics of the Systems

After reviewing the literature and analysing the findings, these latter can be compared and grouped in order to define the results and the critical implementation factors of the six systems. Along with the results and benefits, eight common factors have been found and proposed as shown in the second column from the left in Table 11.1. They are: results and benefits; management style; deployment of the system; employee management, deployment and participation; voice of the customer; tools, techniques and IT; optimisation of the system; day-by-day check and control of the results; review of the system.

All the six systems share customer satisfaction as a common tract. COPQ is pursued in the systems linked to quality such as JTQC, TQM, Deming's, Six Sigma as well as Lean but in different ways. JTQC is focused on quality assurance, TQM and Six Sigma manage COPQ according to Harrington's classification (1986) who divided them into external and internal, these latter further divided into prevention, appraisal and defective costs. Lean considers defectiveness inside the so-called wastes and not-value added activities, and Deming's system linked COPQ to process variation, whereas BPR considers COPQ just one of the costs that can affect profitability. According to Goh (2002), Six Sigma, like BPR, is a very cost-oriented system and it can sometimes sacrifice other results to achieve short-term savings.

BPR needs an 'autocratic' and aggressive management sometimes more oriented to short-term results. TQM and Deming's are the only systems that take care of CSR and the stakeholders as a whole. Management should be involved and participate in all the systems. Deming's is the only system that points out that managers should act like psychologists, trying to improve internal people's potential.

JTQC and Lean share the same typical Japanese way of deploying the system based on hoshin kanri. TQM, Deming's system and BPR do not suggest a precise way of deploying, whereas Six Sigma invented the DMAIC pattern. According to Harry and Schroeder (2000), DMAIC ties up the business level to the operations one and can be followed for long-term goals as well as short-term projects; for the design processes Six Sigma suggests the DFSS system.

A. Chiarini, *From Total Quality Control to Lean Six Sigma*, SpringerBriefs in Business,
DOI: 10.1007/978-88-470-2658-2_11, © The Author(s) 2012

Table 11.1 Results, critical implementation factors and approach to improvements of the six systems

			JTQC	TQM	Deming's	Lean	BPR	Six Sigma
A P	1	Results achieved and benefits	Customer satisfaction and quality assurance	Customer satisfaction, COPQ and CSR performance	Customer satisfaction, staff satisfaction and all the stakeholders	Reduces waste, cost reduction system, particularly increases value added for the customer	Cost reduction system, customer satisfaction, streamline and downsize oriented	Customer satisfaction, cost reduction system, particularly concerning COPQ
	2	Management style	Long-term oriented, management by fact, respect for humanity, participatory management and capacity to involve all the staff	Long-term oriented, management by fact, capacity to involve all the staff, participatory management	Clear view of the system of profound knowledge, long-period oriented, not particularly focused on numerical targets, promoting cooperation and not competition, being a 'psychologist'	Long-term oriented, management by fact, respect for humanity, participatory management and capacity to involve all the staff	'Aggressive' and autocratic top management. Long- and short-term oriented	Long-term oriented, management by fact, capacity to involve all the staff, participatory management
	3	Deployment of the system	*Hoshin kanri*	*Hoshin kanri* and other particular systems for deployment	No particular systems for deployment	*Hoshin kanri*	No particular systems for deployment	Use of a specific DMAIC pattern DFSS within design processes
D	4	Employee management, development and participation	Use of quality control circles. Maximum involvement, respect for humanity, improvement of human potential. Education and training for the best-practices. Extrinsic and intrinsic motivation trade-off	Use of quality control circles and other improvement teams. Maximum involvement. Education and training for the best-practices. Extrinsic and intrinsic motivation trade-off. Training on quality tools and problem solving	Use of quality control circles. Maximum involvement. Cooperative employees rather than competitive. Intrinsic motivation has to be developed. Quality training for reducing variation	Use of Kaizen events. Maximum involvement. Respect for humanity, improvement of human potential. Training on specific tools. Extrinsic and intrinsic motivation trade-off	Use of reengineering teams with a 'Czar' as team leader. People involvement, structured hierarchy. Extrinsic motivation leads people. Training for specialists of mapping and reengineering	Improvement teams, certified yellow and black belts as team leaders. Maximum involvement, structured hierarchy. Extrinsic motivation leads people. Training on quality tools and statistics

(continued)

Table 11.1 (continued)

			JTQC	TQM	Deming's	Lean	BPR	Six Sigma
	5	Voice of the customer	Voice of the customer defined in relation to competition	Voice of the customer defined in relation to competition	Voice of the customer is defined in observance to stakeholders' needs	Voice of the customer is defined for the value added, processes are 'demand driven'	Voice of the customer defined in relation to competition	Voice of the customer defined in relation to competition
	6	Tools and techniques, IT	Typical quality tools (basic, managerial and advanced).Problem Solving, quality audits	Typical quality tools (basic, managerial and advanced). Problem Solving tools	Quality tools are important, even if each organisation choose its own tools based on the theory	Uses specific and well-coded tools invented in the so-called TPS	Tools for analysing and mapping processes, tools for problem solving. IT for mapping and reengineering the processes	Typical quality tools (basic, managerial and advanced). Problem solving and project management tools. IT for managing statistical data
C	7	Optimisation of the system	The entire system should be performed for all the systems	The entire system should be performed for all the systems	The entire system should be performed for all the systems	The entire system should be performed for all the systems	The entire system should be performed for all the systems. Few processes or departments can be affected by reengineering	The entire system should be performed for all the systems
	8	Day-by-day check and control of the results	Non-conformities indicators. Quality audits, status of the corrective and preventive actions	Performance indicators	Performance indicators. No use of targets. Methods are more important than goals	Visual control and management. Performance indicators including Lean metrics	Performance indicators	Performance indicators. Certification of the improvement projects using sigma level and savings
A	9	Review of the system	Quality indicators. Hoshin kanri	Performance indicators. Self-Assessment. Benchmarking	Review of the theory	Hoshin kanri. Performance indicators including Lean metrics	Performance indicators	Performance indicators in particular COPQ

JTQC, Lean and Deming's system point out the importance of the respect for humanity, although Deming's system is particularly focused on win–win situations and cooperation instead of competition. Deming's system in this way emphasises how intrinsic motivations should be more pursued than extrinsic external motivations.

The quality circles suggested by JTQC, TQM and Deming's system as voluntary teams for improvement were sometimes experienced as failures in Western culture. The reasons lie in weak senior managers' leadership and in an unclear connection with company strategies (Hayward et al. 1985; Drago 1988). However, cultural and even religious influences seem to lie in the participatory manner of managing employees. For instance Picken (1987) analysed the influence of the Shinto belief in the innate goodness of human nature and consequently the intrinsic capacity of people to grow; by contrast, in Western societies the worker is expected to perform according to external factors.

According to Table 11.1, voice of customers is surely a common critical implementation factor, even though in Deming's system it should be followed in accordance to all the stakeholders' needs. Lean is particularly demand driven; the orders pull and synchronise all the processes.

Tools and techniques are more or less the same in JTQC, TQM, Deming's system and Six Sigma. They are typical of the quality management world, from the seven basic tools to the advanced statistical ones. Six Sigma projects are often carried out with specific statistical software. Deming's system and Six Sigma promote tools that reduce variation inside processes and Six Sigma contextualises the tools and techniques strictly within the DMAIC pattern. Lean offers personalised tools for reducing wastes and to stream the flow. BPR is based on a massive use of software in order to map, reengineer and standardise the processes.

The entire system should be performed for all the systems, even though BPR, because of its nature, can be used for short-term results inside a few processes or departments. Six Sigma can also be used for short-term results; however, its powerful results in terms of reducing COPQ are normally reached in the long term.

Indicators are the measures to control the day-by-day results in all the systems. JTQC takes into account indicators linked to non-conformities as well as quality audits and corrective-preventive actions. TQM and Six Sigma use COPQ indicators as long as Six Sigma validates the results of the projects measuring the sigma level or variation around the target to be achieved. Lean is more focused on the concept of visual control and promotes its typical indicators such as lead time and OEE. Deming's system cautions about the use of targets as indicators, focusing more on the methods to reach improvements.

The periodical review of the systems in JTQC and Lean Thinking is mainly based on hoshin kanri. TQM introduces the self-assessment and benchmarking process whereas Deming's system tries to understand if the 'theory' which underpins the system is right in terms of stakeholders' satisfaction. BPR stresses the cost reduction results as well as the downsizing of the organisation. Six Sigma wants finance managers to review and certify the COPQ results and the savings in general. Managers sometimes can even have recourse to external certification such as financial auditors and comptrollers.

References

Drago, R. (1988). Quality circle survival: An exploratory analysis. *Industrial Relations: A Journal of Economy and Society, 27*(3), 336–351.

Goh, T. N. (2002). A strategic assessment of six sigma. *Quality and Reliability Engineering International, 18*(5), 403–410.

Harry, M. J., & Schroeder, R. (2000). *The breakthrough management strategy revolutionizing the world's top corporations*. New York: Doubleday.

Hayward, S. G., Dale, B. G., & Fraser, V. C. M. (1985). Quality circle failure and how to avoid it. *European Management Journal, 3*(2), 103–111.

Picken, S. D. B. (1987). Values and value related strategies in Japanese corporate culture. *Journal of Business Ethics, 6*(2), 137–143.

Chapter 12
Lessons Learned from the Comparison and Discussion

Many lessons can be learned from the previous comparison and discussion of the literature review findings.

First, it seems that TQC in Western cultures has evolved into the TQM system losing over time its Japanese style. Some authors have claimed that TQM gurus have sometimes brought confusion to the discussions (Chatterjee and Yilmaz 1993), other authors that several projects have been carried out under the TQM umbrella but with a different approach and results, even claimed that TQM is more a philosophy than a precise science. In any case, looking at Table 11.1 it can be noted how TQM, even if it has lost its identity, maintains the typical quality tools and techniques as does JTQC.

Furthermore, management style, as well as cultural factors, seems to have carried TQM away from Western companies. Deming (1993) listed the mistakes that Western management should avoid in order to implement what is called a System of Profound Knowledge. From Table 11.1 it can be noted how Deming's system has several points in common with JTQC and even with Lean Thinking. However, looking at the very few papers about Deming's system, a lack of interest in this system and probably in its application can be asserted. Deming was one of the fathers of TQM and surely influenced TQM in Japan; despite that, it is not so clear what TQM in Japan has inherited from Deming's System of Profound Knowledge.

From the late 1990s the number of papers dedicated to TQM began to decrease, in the meanwhile some authors claimed that the new 'fad' Six Sigma was borne (Näslund 2008). However, the findings of this paper do not lead in this direction. Six Sigma is not a fad; rather it could be an evolution of systems that have not succeeded in adapting themselves to Western culture, in particular TQM. Indeed like TQM, Six Sigma tries to reduce COPQ, it inherits all the TQM tools but it offers a very structured and measurable pattern, the DMAIC, for improving processes. This is particularly aligned to the Western thought that expects a worker to perform according to external motivations (Picken 1987). By contrast, companies

A. Chiarini, *From Total Quality Control to Lean Six Sigma*, SpringerBriefs in Business, DOI: 10.1007/978-88-470-2658-2_12, © The Author(s) 2012

in Japan believe in the influence of the Shinto belief in the innate goodness of human nature and consequently the intrinsic capacity of people to grow.

From the literature it seems that Six Sigma, especially in the USA, has almost substituted TQM. Nonetheless, how many companies have embraced Six Sigma leaving TQM and in what circumstances this has happened is still uncertain.

BPR was popular during the 1990s basically because companies needed to downsize and better apply IT. Nowadays, the use of IT to support business operations is no longer considered a breakthrough but just a tool and downsizing is just linked to economic crisis, especially in the USA. Looking again the critical implementation factors in Table 11.1, Six Sigma is a hierarchical system, that orients employee management towards external motivations rather than intrinsic, and it can also be used instead of BPR in the short-period for getting aggressive savings.

In the literature written in English there is no trace of Six Sigma application in Japanese companies. TQM in the Japanese style is still implemented even though is not so clear what are the differences, if any, from the original JTQC and how it has been evolving since.

JTQC and Deming's system seem to share some critical implementation factors with Lean as well. This is in part taken for granted considering the same Japanese origin. In fact from the Table 11.1 it can be noted how JTQC shares critical factors such as the use of hoshin kanri deployment, and the same way of managing employees in terms of respect for humanity, improvement of human potential as well as quick voluntary teams similar to quality circles. This is particularly claimed in the original Japanese works of Ohno (1988) and Shingo (1989).

Combining the 'speed' introduced by Lean and the Six Sigma capability of reducing variation, Lean Six Sigma seems to be a well-established system as confirmed by several authors (George 2002; Arnheiter and Maleyeff 2005; Kumar et al. 2006; Wedgwood 2006). However, from a review of the literature concerning Lean Six Sigma, it seems that the critical implementation factors of Lean shared with JTQC are not taken into account or minimised, only the generic involvement of people is underlined in Lean Six Sigma. Dozens of providers that propose a Lean Six Sigma based certification for Black and Green Belts can be found on the Internet. However, these courses look like a Six Sigma—DMAIC course enriched with Lean tools and techniques. Unfortunately neither in the academic literature nor in professional training are there specific references to how to balance and emphasise the intrinsic factors that can grow people's potential.

References

Arnheiter, E. D., & Maleyeff, J. (2005). The integration of lean management and six sigma. *The TQM Magazine, 17*(1), 5–18.

Chatterjee, S., & Yilmaz, M. (1993). Quality confusion: Too many gurus, not enough disciples. *Business Horizons, 36*(3), 15–18.

Deming, W.E. (1993). *The new economics: For industry, Government, Education*. Cambridge, MA: MIT, center for advanced engineering study.

George, M. (2002). *Lean six sigma: Combining six sigma quality with lean production speed*. New York: McGraw-Hill.

Kumar, M., Antony, J., Singhc, R. K., Tiwarid, M. K., & Perry, D. (2006). Implementing the lean sigma framework in an Indian SME: A case study. *Production Planning & Control, 17*(4), 407–423.

Näslund, D. (2008). Lean, six sigma and lean sigma: Fads or real process improvement methods? *Business Process Management Journal, 14*(3), 269–287.

Ohno, T. (1988). *Toyota production system: Beyond large scale production*. Cambridge, MA: Productivity Press.

Picken, S. D. B. (1987). Values and value related strategies in Japanese corporate culture. *Journal of Business Ethics, 6*(2), 137–143.

Shingo, S. (1989). *A study of the Toyota production system from an industrial engineering viewpoint*. Cambridge, MA: Productivity Press.

Wedgwood, I. (2006). *Lean sigma, a practitioner's guide*. Upper Saddle River, NJ: Prentice Hall.

Chapter 13
Conclusions

In this book, literature concerning six important management systems has been reviewed in order to understand what the results achieved by the systems and the critical implementation factors of each of them are. The results and the critical implementation factors have been grouped in Table 11.1 using the PDCA cycle, showing thus a possible way of implementing the systems. Furthermore, the comparison and discussion of the findings shown in Table 11.1 has led to important conclusions and remarks.

First it seems that in Western cultures TQC has evolved into the TQM system gradually losing its Japanese style. Nowadays TQM has lost its identity but it maintains the typical quality tools and techniques of JTQC.

Deming's System of Profound Knowledge is an interesting guideline for Western managers, however, it has had less success than JTQC, TQM and the other systems in the literature. Even the influence of Deming's system on the current Japanese TQM is unclear.

From the end of 1990s Six Sigma seems to have gradually substituted TQM especially in US companies, even if there is no trace of Six Sigma applications in Japan. Six Sigma has a more hierarchical approach and for managing people extrinsic motivations are followed more than intrinsic ones. Six Sigma could also substitute BPR. In fact a short-term aggressive reengineering project could be managed with Six Sigma—DMAIC.

Last but not least the 'marriage' between the Japanese Lean and the American Six Sigma systems has brought a new acclaimed management system. However, from the review of the literature Lean Six Sigma seems more like a DMAIC enriched with Lean tools rather than a Six Sigma in which the Japanese style of managing people is strongly taken into account.

A. Chiarini, *From Total Quality Control to Lean Six Sigma*, SpringerBriefs in Business,
DOI: 10.1007/978-88-470-2658-2_13,

Chapter 14
Agenda for Future Research

This book presents some limits mainly due to the fact that is based on a literature review. Thence, first of all, practitioners and academics could carry out case studies inside companies that have applied all the six systems or the majority of them. Critical implementation factors presented in Table 11.1 need to be validated and eventually put under discussion.

In addition this book enters in the open debate of TQM in Western companies. Surely TQM has lost its popularity, but for what reasons? Has Six Sigma gradually substituted TQM in the West because is more suitable for that culture? There is too much theoretical research, the scientific community needs more case studies concerning companies that have embraced Six Sigma and left TQM. Using a survey within a sample of companies and by the means of quantitative inquiries the hypotheses of a changeover from TQM to Six Sigma could be validated. Furthermore BPR practitioners could analyse whether the DMAIC pattern can perform in alternative aggressive and short-term oriented reengineering projects. Another interesting question arises from this paper. Is there an interest concerning Six Sigma in Japan? Or do Japanese companies continue implementing, as emerged from some literature, TQM in their own style? How far is this latter system from the original JTQC? It could be useful if Japanese practitioners and academics participated more in this debate proposing Japanese case studies as well as general research.

And what about Deming's System of Profound Knowledge? Academics could analyse whether or not it has left something to be inherited, for instance by Six Sigma. Practitioners could analyse successful case studies of Deming's system implementation along with some of the other systems.

Finally Lean Six Sigma needs more investigation from academics and practitioners because the degree of influence of the Japanese style on Six Sigma is unclear. Is it just a matter of integrating tools and techniques or could it finally be the way to introduce to Western culture what JTQC, TQM and Deming's system seems not to have achieved?

A. Chiarini, *From Total Quality Control to Lean Six Sigma*, SpringerBriefs in Business,
DOI: 10.1007/978-88-470-2658-2_14, © The Author(s) 2012

MIX
Papier aus verantwortungsvollen Quellen
Paper from responsible sources
FSC® C105338

If you have any concerns about our products,
you can contact us on
ProductSafety@springernature.com

In case Publisher is established outside the EU,
the EU authorized representative is:
Springer Nature Customer Service Center GmbH
Europaplatz 3, 69115 Heidelberg, Germany

Printed by Libri Plureos GmbH
in Hamburg, Germany